THE BEGINNER'S ROADMAP TO RENTAL PROPERTY INVESTING SUCCESS

A Step-by-Step Guide to Finding, Funding, and Managing Your First Rental Property to Build Wealth and Achieve Financial Freedom

4

Copyright © by James T. Colson 2024. All rights reserved.

Before this document is duplicated or reproduced in any manner, the publisher's consent must be gained. Therefore, the contents within can neither be stored electronically, transferred, nor kept in a database. Neither in Part nor full can the document be copied, scanned, faxed, or retained without approval from the publisher or creator.

TABLE OF CONTENTS

Chapter 1: Understanding the Basics of Rental Property Investing

1.1 What is Rental Property Investing?

1.2 Why Invest in Rental Properties?

1.3 Key Terms and Concepts to Know

Chapter 2: Setting Your Financial Goals

2.1 Defining Your Investment Objectives

2.2 Understanding Cash Flow and ROI

2.3 Setting a Realistic Budget

Chapter 3: Researching and Analyzing the Market

3.1 Identifying Promising Locations

3.2 Understanding Market Trends

3.3 Conducting Comparative Market Analysis (CMA)

Chapter 4: Finding the Right Property

4.1 Types of Rental Properties

4.2 Working with Real Estate Agents

4.3 Evaluating Potential Properties

Chapter 5: Securing Financing for Your Investment

5.1 Understanding Your Financing Options

5.2 Preparing Your Financial Documents

5.3 Getting Pre-Approved for a Loan

Chapter 6: Conducting Due Diligence

6.1 Property Inspections and Appraisals

6.2 Assessing Legal and Zoning Issues

6.3 Calculating Renovation and Repair Costs

Chapter 7: Making an Offer and Closing the Deal

7.1 Crafting a Competitive Offer

7.2 Negotiating the Purchase Price

7.3 Navigating the Closing Process

Chapter 8: Preparing Your Property for Tenants

8.1 Renovations and Upgrades

8.2 Setting the Right Rent Price

8.3 Marketing Your Rental Property

Chapter 9: Managing Your Rental Property

9.1 Finding and Screening Tenants

9.2 Handling Lease Agreements and Security Deposits

9.3 Managing Repairs and Maintenance

Chapter 10: Building Wealth and Expanding Your Portfolio

10.1 Reinvesting Your Profits

10.2 Scaling Up: Acquiring Additional Properties

10.3 Long-Term Strategies for Financial Freedom

UNDERSTANDING THE BASICS OF RENTAL PROPERTY INVESTING

What is Rental Property Investing?

Rental property investing is a powerful wealth-building method that enables people to earn money, diversify their investment portfolio, and eventually attain financial independence. At its essence, rental property investing entails purchasing real estate holdings with the goal of renting them out to tenants who pay rent on a regular basis. This consistent stream of rental income, along with the possibility of the property's value increasing over time, makes rental property investing an appealing option for people trying to build wealth and protect their financial future.

Concept of Rental Income

The main principle behind rental property investing is to generate cash from tenants' rent payments. When you own a rental property, you essentially become a landlord, with your tenants paying you for the opportunity to reside there. This rent is often paid on a monthly basis and serves as the foundation of your cash flow—the money left over after you've paid for all property-related obligations.

The key to successful rental property investing is producing positive cash flow, which occurs when rental income exceeds property expenses. These costs could include mortgage payments, property taxes, insurance, upkeep, and property management fees. When your rental revenue exceeds these expenses, you'll have a profit that you can reinvest, save, or utilize to fund other financial goals.

Appreciation: Real Estate's Long-Term Value

In addition to earning rental income, rental property investing has the possibility for appreciation—a rise in the property's value over time. Real estate markets tend to appreciate when demand for housing rises and the supply of available properties becomes scarce. When your property's value rises, you gain equity, which is the difference between its current market worth and the amount you owe on your mortgage.

For example, if you buy a house for $200,000 and it increases in value to $250,000 over time, you will have $50,000 in equity. This equity can be leveraged in a variety of ways, including selling the home for a profit, refinancing the mortgage to access cash, or using it as security for future investments.

Power of Leverage

One of the most significant benefits of rental property investing is the potential to leverage your money. Leverage is the use of borrowed money to finance the acquisition of a property, allowing you to acquire a valuable asset with a modest amount of your own money. This is commonly accomplished through a mortgage, in which you put down a portion of the property's value and borrow the remainder from a lender.

Leverage increases your potential returns because you generate rental income and benefit from appreciation across the entire property value, not just the portion you paid for with your own money. For example, if you buy a $200,000 house with a 20% down payment ($40,000) and the property appreciates by 10%, the value will rise to $220,000. You have effectively gained $20,000 in equity, representing a 50% return on your initial $40,000 investment.

However, using leverage increases your risk because you are responsible for repaying the debt regardless of how well the property performs. If the rental income does not meet your mortgage payments, or if the property's value falls, you may encounter financial difficulties. That is why it is critical to thoroughly evaluate your investment and verify that you can manage the risks connected with leverage.

Understanding the many types of rental properties

Rental property investing is not a one-size-fits-all strategy; there are numerous sorts of rental properties to invest in, each with its own set of benefits and drawbacks. Understanding these possibilities will allow you to make more educated selections that are consistent with your financial goals and risk tolerance.

- Single-Family Homes: These are freestanding residential properties intended for a single household.

Single-family houses are sometimes the easiest form of rental property for beginners to manage because they require less upkeep and attract long-term tenants, such as families. However, they come with the risk of vacancy—if your renter leaves, your rental revenue is nothing until you locate a new tenant.

- Multi-Family Properties: Duplexes, triplexes, and apartment buildings are examples of multi-unit properties. Multi-family homes provide the benefit of many income streams from various tenants, lowering the chance of total vacancy. They also provide for economies of scale, as maintenance and management costs can be dispersed across multiple units. However, managing multifamily residences can be more difficult and time-consuming.

- Short-Term Rental: Short-term rental properties, such as holiday homes or Airbnb rentals, can generate more money than long-term rentals. Short-term rentals are especially profitable in famous tourist attractions or locations with a high demand for temporary lodging. However, they require more active management, such as frequent cleaning, guest turnover, and adherence to local standards.

- Commercial Property: Although more advanced, investing in commercial rental properties, such as office buildings, retail spaces, and warehouses, can result in higher income and longer lease terms. Commercial tenants frequently sign leases for multiple years, ensuring consistent cash flow. However, commercial real estate necessitates a more in-depth understanding of market dynamics and often involves greater initial investments.

Example: A First-Time Investor's Journey.

Let us consider Sarah, a first-time rental property investor. Sarah chose to buy a single-family home in a burgeoning suburban neighborhood. She thoroughly investigated the market and discovered a neighborhood with a high demand for rental units due to its closeness to good schools and job prospects.

Sarah saw a house advertised for $180,000 and obtained finance with a 20% down payment of $36,000. Her overall investment, including closing expenses and minor modifications, was $40,000. Sarah calculated that the property might yield $1,500 in monthly rent, with expenses reaching $1,200, resulting in a $300 monthly positive cash flow.

Over the next five years, the property's value soared to $220,000, and Sarah's equity grew as she paid down the mortgage. Sarah generated rental revenue while also building significant equity, laying the groundwork for future investments.

Why Invest in Rental Properties?

Investing in rental homes is a popular approach for those looking to generate long-term wealth and financial security. Unlike other types of investments, rental properties provide a unique blend of income generation, prospective appreciation, and tangible assets that can give both stability and growth. Whether you want to supplement your income, save for retirement, or achieve financial independence, rental property investing is a fascinating prospect.

Creating Passive Income

One of the most tempting parts of rental property investing is the possibility to earn passive income. Rental properties are a good source of passive income, which is money earned without actively working for it. When you own a rental property, renters pay you rent on a monthly basis, giving a constant and stable income source.

This money might be especially important because it is not dependent on your time or work, unlike a regular job. As long as you have renters in your property, you are making money, which can provide you with greater financial freedom and stability. As you acquire more homes, this revenue will increase, allowing you to reach greater financial freedom.

For example, suppose you own a single-family rental home that earns $1,500 per month in rent. After paying your mortgage, property taxes, insurance, and upkeep, you'll have $400 in positive cash flow per month. That's $4,800 in extra revenue every year, which you might reinvest in other homes, save for future costs, or utilize to upgrade your lifestyle.

Appreciation and Wealth Building

Beyond the immediate benefit of passive income, rental properties have the potential to generate enormous wealth through appreciation. Real estate values typically rise over time, particularly in markets with rising populations, robust economies, and limited housing supply. As the value of your property rises, so does your equity—the amount of the property you own wholly, which can be an effective instrument for accumulating long-term assets.

Consider the following scenario: you buy a rental property for $200,000. Over the following decade, the property will rise at an average rate of 3% each year, bringing its value to around $268,000. During this period, you've also been paying down your mortgage, boosting your equity. By the end of the decade, you'll have not only received rental income but also gained $68,000 in equity, representing a significant return on your initial investment.

This appreciation might lead to new options, such as refinancing your house to free up funds for additional investments or selling the property at a profit to reinvest in a more profitable market. The potential for gain makes rental property investing an appealing alternative for people seeking to build wealth over time.

Tax advantages

Rental property investors can also benefit from a number of tax breaks that can greatly increase the profitability of their properties. The United States tax code provides various deductions and perks expressly for real estate investors, allowing you to keep more of your income while lowering your tax bill.

One of the most significant tax advantages is the opportunity to deduct expenses associated with your rental property. These expenses may include mortgage interest, property taxes, insurance, repairs, maintenance, and even property management fees. By deducting these expenses, you effectively reduce your taxable income, which can lead to significant tax savings.

Depreciation is another big tax benefit. Depreciation permits you to deduct a portion of the property's worth each year as if it were losing value over time, even if it is actually increasing. This deduction can be used to offset rental income, lowering your overall tax payment. For example, if your property is worth $200,000 and the land is worth $50,000, you can depreciate the remaining $150,000 over 27.5 years, giving in an annual deduction of almost $5,450.

Furthermore, if you decide to sell your rental property, you may be eligible for capital gains tax breaks, which are often lower than regular income tax rates. If you own the property for more than a year, the earnings from its sale may be taxed at long-term capital gains rates, possibly saving you thousands of dollars in taxes.

Hedge Against Inflation

Investing in rental properties also provides a natural hedge against inflation, which is an important aspect in any long-term investing strategy. Inflation gradually erodes money's purchasing power, causing the cost of goods and services to rise. However, real estate often appreciates at a faster rate than inflation, allowing your investment to remain or even rise in value in real terms.

Furthermore, if inflation rises, so will rental prices. Landlords can often raise rents over time to keep up with inflation, ensuring that their rental income maintains purchasing power. This option to change rents makes rental properties an especially robust investment during periods of economic uncertainty or rising inflation.

For example, if inflation causes a 3% annual increase in the cost of living, you may be able to raise your rentals by the same amount each year. If your property first rents for $1,500 per month, after five years of 3% yearly rent increases, your monthly rent may rise to around $1,740. This rise not only maintains your income's purchasing power, but it also increases your overall return on investment.

A Tangible Asset With Intrinsic Value

Unlike stocks and bonds, rental properties are real assets with inherent worth. You can see, touch, and improve your property, giving you greater control over your investment. This tangibility provides a level of protection that other types of investment may not supply, particularly during periods of economic turbulence.

Owning a rental property implies you have a physical asset that may be used in a variety of ways. If the rental market changes, you may consider selling the property, repurposing it for personal use, or even converting it to a different sort of rental (for example, a short-term holiday rental). The flexibility and security that come with owning a real asset make rental properties an adaptable and dependable investment option.

For example, during a stock market slump, your rental property may continue to generate stable rental income, acting as a buffer against losses in other sections of your portfolio. Furthermore, if you decide to upgrade the property—for example, by upgrading the kitchen or adding a bathroom—you will instantly boost its value and rental potential, increasing the profitability of your investment.

Building Generational Wealth

Investing in rental properties is more than just safeguarding your financial future; it also means leaving a legacy for future generations. Rental properties can be passed down to your children or other heirs, giving them a source of income and financial stability. This wealth transfer can assist ensure that your family continues to profit from your investments even after you are gone.

By carefully managing and developing your rental property portfolio, you can leave a legacy that will benefit your family's financial well-being for decades. This concept of generational wealth is especially powerful in real estate, where holdings can continue to rise in value and create income, offering ongoing benefits to your heirs.

Consider leaving behind a portfolio of well-managed rental properties that provide continuous income for your children and grandchildren. This money might be used to pay for education, start new businesses, or create a financial safety net, allowing them to pursue their own financial objectives. In this approach, rental property investing becomes more than just a vehicle to acquire personal wealth; it also serves to empower future generations.

Key Terms and Concepts to Know

Understanding the basic terminologies and concepts is critical as you begin your rental property investment journey. These fundamental features will not only help you traverse the world of real estate with confidence, but they will also allow you to make informed decisions that will improve your investment performance. A strong understanding of these topics is essential for evaluating possible properties, analyzing negotiations, and managing your investments.

Cash flow

Any rental property venture relies heavily on cash flow. It represents the amount of money left over each month after all income and costs are taken into consideration. In other words, cash flow is the profit that remains after deducting mortgage payments, property taxes, insurance, maintenance, and other operating expenses.

Positive cash flow happens when the rental property's income exceeds its expenses. This is an important indicator of a successful investment since it shows that the property is not only self-sustaining but also generates additional income. For example, if you rent out a house for $2,000 per month and have total monthly expenses of $1,500, you will generate $500 in cash flow.

On the other hand, negative cash flow occurs when the property's expenses exceed its revenue. This arrangement might be financially exhausting, and you may need to augment the property's bills out of pocket. As a result, each rental property investor's primary goal should be to generate positive cash flow.

Capitalization Rate (cap rate)

The capitalization rate, sometimes known as the cap rate, is a fundamental indicator for determining the prospective return on a real estate investment. It is determined by dividing the property's annual net operating income (NOI) by its current market value or acquisition price. The cap rate provides an indication of the property's profitability and is frequently used to compare various investment options.

For example, if a property earns $50,000 in annual NOI and is worth $500,000, the cap rate would be 10%. A greater cap rate typically signifies a larger return on investment, but it can also indicate increased risk. A lower cap rate may indicate a more steady investment with lesser returns.

Understanding cap rates is critical for determining whether a property matches your investing objectives. While a 10% cap rate may seem enticing, it's necessary to weigh the risks and determine whether the property's location, condition, and tenant stability worth the possible return.

Net Operating Income (NOI)

Net operating income (NOI) is an important concept in rental property investing. It is the entire income earned by a property after deducting all operational costs but before accounting for mortgage payments and taxes. NOI is used to determine a property's profitability and is an important factor in calculating the cap rate.

For example, if a rental property earns $100,000 in gross rental income and incurs $30,000 in running costs (including maintenance, property management fees, and utilities), the NOI is $70,000. This statistic is important since it represents the property's genuine earning potential, disregarding finance expenditures.

NOI is also utilized in a variety of computations, including evaluating the property's value using the income approach and analyzing its ability to meet debt payments. A high NOI implies a profitable property that can generate continuous income and sustain long-term investment growth.

Loan-to-Value Ratio (LTV)

The Loan-to-worth (LTV) ratio is a financial term that represents the relationship between a loan amount and a property's appraised worth. Lenders use the LTV ratio to determine the risk of lending to a borrower; the greater the LTV, the riskier the loan is.

For example, if you buy a $400,000 house and get a loan for $300,000, your LTV ratio is 75%. A lower LTV ratio, such as 70%, shows that you're borrowing less than the property's value, which might lead to better loan terms, such as a reduced interest rate.

Understanding LTV ratios is vital because they influence your financing alternatives and the amount of equity you have in the property. A lower LTV ratio indicates more equity, lowering the lender's risk and potentially leading to better lending terms.

Equity

Equity refers to the portion of the property's value that you own wholly, free of any mortgages or other liens. It indicates your financial stake in the property, which might increase over time due to mortgage payments and property appreciation.

For example, if you buy a $300,000 home with a $60,000 down payment and a $240,000 mortgage, you'll start with $60,000 in equity. As you pay down your mortgage and the house appreciates, your equity grows. If the property's value increases to $350,000 and you pay off $50,000 of the mortgage, your equity will be $160,000.

Equity is a valuable asset in real estate investing because it may be used to fund additional property purchases, repairs, or even as a financial buffer in times of need. The more equity you accumulate, the better your financial flexibility and security.

Depreciation

Depreciation is a tax benefit that allows rental property owners to deduct the cost of the property's value over time, accounting for the property's natural wear and tear. While the property may increase in value, the IRS permits you to deduct depreciation as a non-cash expense, which can dramatically lower your taxable income.

For residential rental properties, the IRS usually permits you to depreciate the property's value (excluding the land) over 27.5 years. For example, if you buy a rental property for $275,000 and the land is worth $75,000, you can depreciate the remaining $200,000 over 27.5 years, resulting in an annual depreciation deduction of almost $7,273.

Depreciation can have a considerable influence on your entire tax liability, making it one of the most beneficial tax breaks for real estate investors. Depreciation can boost cash flow and profitability by lowering taxable income.

Appreciation

Appreciation is the growth in the value of a property over time. This is one of the key ways real estate investors accumulate money, as assets tend to appreciate as a result of inflation, demand, and improvements to the property or surrounding area.

For example, if you buy a property for $200,000 and it improves in value to $250,000 over five years, you'll have made $50,000 in appreciation. This gain in value can be realized by selling the property, refinancing it, or using the increased equity to buy more properties.

The local economy, housing market conditions, and property upgrades all have an impact on appreciation. While it is not guaranteed, historical trends indicate that real estate increases with time, making it an important part of any investing strategy.

CapEx (capital expenditures)

Capital Expenditures, or CapEx, are the cash spent by an investor to buy, improve, or maintain a property. These are often major investments that extend the property's life and increase its value, such as repairing a roof, installing a new HVAC system, or renovating a kitchen.

For example, if you spend $10,000 on a new roof, this is considered capital expenditure. These expenses must be considered when determining the profitability of your property because they can have an impact on your cash flow and ROI.

Unlike normal maintenance charges, CapEx costs are usually stretched out across several years. Budgeting for CapEx is critical for maintaining the property's value and making it appealing to tenants.

GRM (Gross Rent Multiplier)

The Gross Rent Multiplier (GRM) is a simple tool for estimating the value of a rental property in relation to its rental income. It is determined by dividing the property's price by its annual gross rental income. The GRM allows you to quickly evaluate properties and determine whether they are reasonably priced based on their revenue potential.

For example, if a home is offered for $300,000 and earns $30,000 in annual rental income, the GRM is 10. A lower GRM shows that the property is overvalued in comparison to its rental income, whereas a greater GRM may indicate that the property is expensive.

While the GRM is a good place to start, when assessing an investment, you should also consider operational expenses, location, and property quality. The GRM does not account for these variables, hence it should be used in conjunction with other measures.

Return On Investment (ROI)

Return on Investment (ROI) is an important indicator of the profitability of an investment. It is computed by dividing the investment's total profit by its initial cost. ROI in rental property investing can be measured on two different bases: cash-on-cash and total return.

For example, if you invest $50,000 in a rental property and earn $5,000 in annual net profit, your ROI will be 10%. This means you receive 10% of your initial investment each year, which is a good indication of the property's profitability.

ROI is an important indicator for comparing investment options and determining whether a property matches your financial objectives. A greater ROI suggests a more successful investment, but it is also crucial to assess the risks and the long-term viability of the returns.

SETTING YOUR Financial Goals

Defining Your Investment Objectives

When it comes to rental property investing, setting your investment goals is the first crucial step toward financial success. Your goals will dictate every decision you make, from finding the perfect properties to maintaining your portfolio. A clear knowledge of your goals will not only keep you motivated, but will also allow you to track your progress along the way. This chapter delves into the numerous aspects of establishing investment objectives that are consistent with your personal and financial goals.

Understanding your "Why"

Before getting into the specifics of your investment goals, it's critical to understand your underlying reasons for investing in rental homes. Knowing your "why" will provide you direction and purpose, allowing you to remain dedicated even when faced with adversity. Your motivations could range from increasing wealth to reaching financial independence, leaving a legacy for your family, or establishing a passive income stream.

For example, if your primary goal is to retire early, your investment plan would most likely revolve around acquiring properties that provide significant cash flow, allowing you to replace your present income. If you're motivated by the goal to create generational wealth, you may prioritize long-term appreciation and the opportunity to pass valuable assets down to your successors.

Understanding your "why" will not only influence your investment goals, but will also help you make decisions that are consistent with your long-term vision. It serves as the cornerstone for your overall investing strategy.

Short-Term Versus Long-Term Goals

Determining your investing objectives necessitates a clear difference between short-term and long-term goals. Both are crucial, but they serve different functions and necessitate distinct approaches. Short-term goals are often milestones that you hope to attain within the next one to five years, and long-term goals are those you intend to achieve over a decade or more.

For example, a short-term aim could be to buy your first rental property within the following year. This objective is explicit, quantifiable, and time-bound, giving you a clear target to strive toward. To accomplish this, you must focus on increasing your funds, boosting your credit score, and locating possible properties that fit your budget.

Long-term objectives, on the other hand, may include accumulating a portfolio of five to ten homes over the following two decades or reaching a point where your rental income fully supports your living expenditures. These objectives necessitate a larger view, centered on strategic planning, market research, and ongoing property management.

Balancing short-term and long-term goals is critical for keeping momentum and ensuring that your current actions contribute to your overall vision. While short-term goals keep you motivated and on track, long-term goals provide a broader perspective that influences your overall investment plan.

Risk Tolerance and Investment Style

Understanding your risk tolerance and selecting an investment strategy that matches it is also an important part of determining your investment objectives. Risk tolerance refers to your aptitude and readiness to accept probable losses in the quest of profits. It is a personal issue determined by your financial status, investment experience, and psychological tolerance for risk.

For example, if you have a low risk tolerance, you may want to invest in homes in stable, high-demand districts, where the chance of vacancy or substantial market changes is reduced. These properties may have lesser returns, but they give more stable income with less volatility.

If you have a higher risk tolerance, you may be willing to invest in emerging markets or distressed properties that offer larger returns. While these investments carry a higher risk, they also provide prospects for large appreciation and cash flow.

Your investment style, whether conservative, moderate, or aggressive, should correspond to your risk tolerance. A conservative investor may prefer properties with lower cap rates but more stability, whereas an adventurous investor may seek out properties with higher cap rates in less established areas. Understanding this balance will allow you to make investing decisions that are in line with your comfort level and financial objectives.

Establishing Specific, Measurable, Achievable, Relevant, and Time-bound (SMART) Goals

Once you've recognized your reasons, balanced your short- and long-term goals, and determined your risk tolerance, it's time to put these insights into action. The SMART framework is an effective tool for this process, allowing you to define goals that are Specific, Measurable, Achievable, Relevant, and Time-bound.

Instead of creating a general goal such as "I want to make money from rental properties," a SMART goal would be "I will purchase my first rental property within the next 12 months that generates a minimum monthly cash flow of $500 after all expenses." This goal is explicit (buying a rental property), measurable (at least $500 in income flow), attainable (based on market research and your financial circumstances), relevant (aligned with your overall investing objectives), and time-bound (within 12 months).

SMART goals provide clarity and direction, ensuring that your investment activities are in line with your overall objectives. They also make it easier to monitor your progress and make changes as necessary.

Aligning Goals and Your Financial Situation

Defining your investment objectives also entails matching your goals to your present financial status. It's critical to be realistic about what you can achieve given your income, savings, credit score, and general financial situation.

For example, if you're just starting out and have limited money, your first goal could be to save for a down payment on a single rental property. As your finances improve, you can set more ambitious goals, such as purchasing numerous houses or investing in higher-value real estate.

It's also crucial to think about the financial ramifications of your investment goals, such as how they can affect your cash flow, tax liabilities, and overall financial stability. For example, if you want to maximize cash flow, you can look for properties with lower purchase prices and more rental income, which can bring immediate financial benefits but may come at the expense of future appreciation potential.

By matching your goals with your financial condition, you can set realistic, attainable goals that will help you get closer to financial freedom without overextending yourself or taking unnecessary risks.

Revisit and Adjust Your Goals

Finally, remember that your investment goals are not written in stone. As your financial circumstances, market conditions, and personal ambitions change, you must examine and adapt your objectives accordingly. Flexibility is critical for long-term success in rental property investing.

For example, if you set a goal of acquiring five rental properties within ten years and market conditions or your financial status change, you may need to adapt your timeline or the types of properties you're looking for. Alternatively, if you meet your goals sooner than intended, you may create new, more aggressive targets to continue expanding your portfolio.

Regularly analyzing and revising your goals ensures that they remain relevant to your present position and long-term ambition. It also enables you to be proactive in responding to changes and capturing new possibilities as they arise.

Understanding Cash Flow And ROI.

A thorough understanding of cash flow and return on investment (ROI) is required for effective rental property investing. These financial parameters constitute the foundation of your investment strategy, guiding your decisions and allowing you to evaluate the performance of your properties. Understanding cash flow and ROI, as well as how to optimize them, will allow you to make informed decisions that correspond with your financial objectives and maximize the potential of your investment.

What is cash flow?

Cash flow in rental property investing is the net amount of money earned from a property after all expenses have been paid. It's a key measure of your property's financial health and capacity to create passive revenue. Positive cash flow means that rental income exceeds expenses, however negative cash flow means that you are spending more than you are generating.

For example, if you own a rental property that earns $2,000 per month in rental income but has monthly expenses of $1,500 (mortgage payments, property taxes, insurance, maintenance, and property management fees), your monthly cash flow is $500. This $500 represents your monthly profit, which you can reinvest, save, or utilize to meet other financial goals.

Cash flow is important since it directly affects your ability to maintain and grow your real estate holdings. Properties with significant positive cash flow give a cushion against unexpected expenses, market downturns, and vacancies, ensuring that your investment is profitable in the long run.

Maximizing cash flow

Maximizing cash flow necessitates close attention to

both revenue and expenses. Setting competitive but realistic rent prices is critical for income generation. Conducting extensive market research to see what comparable houses in the region are renting for will assist you in striking the perfect balance between attracting renters and optimizing rental income. Offering desired amenities or making strategic improvements to the property can help justify higher rents, increasing your revenue flow.

On the expense side, competent property management is critical. Keeping maintenance and repair costs under control, getting advantageous insurance rates, and reducing vacancies through aggressive tenant retention measures can all help you save money. Furthermore, refinancing your mortgage to get a lower interest rate or extending the loan term might reduce your monthly mortgage payments, increasing your cash flow.

Consider a home with an initial mortgage payment of $1,200 per month and a 5% interest rate. If you refinance at a 3.5% interest rate, your new mortgage payment might be reduced to $1,000 per month, immediately enhancing your cash flow by $200 per month. This seemingly minor change can have a major influence on your total financial situation and ability to reinvest in new homes.

What is ROI?

Return on Investment (ROI) is a profitability metric stated as a percentage of the initial investment cost. In rental property investing, ROI is computed by dividing the property's annual net profit by the total amount spent, which includes the purchase price, closing charges, and any renovation expenses.

For example, if you buy a rental property for $200,000, invest $20,000 on repairs, and make an annual net profit of $15,000, your ROI will be computed as follows:

To calculate ROI, multiply (Annual Net Profit / Total Investment) by 100. For example, $15,000 divided by $220,000 yields 6.82% ROI.

This 6.82% ROI illustrates how well your investment generates profit in comparison to the amount invested. A higher ROI indicates a more profitable investment; hence it is an important indicator for evaluating possible assets and comparing different investment options.

Factors affecting ROI

Several factors can affect your ROI, including property location, purchase price, financing terms, and operational costs. Choosing properties in regions with high rental demand, limited supply, and potential for appreciation might help you maximize your ROI. Furthermore, negotiating a good purchase price or obtaining low-interest financing might lower your initial investment while improving your return.

Operating expenses also play an important part in calculating ROI. These expenses include property management fees, maintenance expenditures, insurance, property taxes, and utilities. Keeping these expenses under control is critical for maximizing your ROI. For example, choosing a fixed-rate mortgage can give consistency in monthly payments, allowing you to better manage your cash flow and safeguard your ROI from interest rate changes.

To illustrate, consider two identical properties in separate locations: Property A is in a high-demand metropolitan region with a $300,000 purchase price, but Property B is in a less competitive suburban area with a $250,000. If both properties earn the same annual net profit of $20,000, Property B will have a greater ROI due to the lower original investment:

Property A ROI: ($20,000 / $300,000) 100 = 6.67%.
Property B ROI equals ($20,000 / $250,000). 100 = 8%

In this case, Property B provides a higher return on investment despite the fact that both properties create the same net profit.

Balancing Cash Flow with ROI

While both cash flow and ROI are vital, they serve distinct functions and may need trade-offs. A property with high cash flow may have a poorer ROI if the acquisition price was high or significant capital was invested up front. In contrast, a property with a high ROI may create less cash flow if it is located in a less expensive neighborhood with lower rental demand.

Balancing these two indicators entails matching them to your entire financial objectives and investing plan. If your primary goal is to create immediate money, concentrating on properties with a significant positive cash flow may be preferable. On the other side, if you want to accumulate money over time through property appreciation, a larger ROI may be more important.

For example, a young investor with a high risk tolerance and a long investment horizon may prioritize assets with a high ROI potential, even if the cash flow is minimal. Over time, the appreciation of the property's value and rising rental income might greatly increase their fortune. In contrast, a retiree may select homes with constant, positive cash flow to assure a consistent income source that supports their lifestyle.

Use Cash Flow and ROI to Make Investment Decisions

Understanding cash flow and ROI is critical to making sound investment decisions. These measurements provide vital insights into a property's financial performance, allowing you to determine whether it meets your financial objectives and risk tolerance.

For example, before acquiring a home, you can calculate its prospective cash flow and ROI using expected rental revenue and expenses. This study can help you decide if the property is a good fit for your portfolio and fulfills your investment criteria.

Furthermore, continuously analyzing the cash flow and ROI of your existing properties allows you to identify areas for improvement, such as raising rents, lowering expenses, or refinancing. It also allows you to evaluate the overall performance of your portfolio and make necessary adjustments to meet your financial objectives.

By grasping the principles of cash flow and ROI, you'll be able to make strategic investment decisions that maximize returns, reduce risks, and help you achieve financial independence through rental property ownership.

Setting A Realistic Budget

Setting a reasonable budget is an important step toward successful rental property investing. A well-thought-out budget not only guarantees that you have the financial resources to manage your assets, but it also assists you in avoiding frequent traps that might derail your progress. By taking a proactive approach to budgeting, you can position yourself for success and make solid financial decisions that match with your objectives.

Understanding the Components of a Rental Property Budget

A complete rental property budget consists of several major components, each of which is critical to the overall financial sustainability of the investment. These components include the initial purchase price, continuing operational expenditures, and contingency cash for unforeseen situations. Understanding these factors and how they interact will allow you to establish a budget that is both realistic and sustainable.

When calculating initial purchase costs, it is critical to account more than simply the purchase price of the property. Closing costs, including as appraisals, inspections, legal fees, and title insurance, should also be considered. These expenditures can quickly build up, surprising new investors who are unprepared for the added expenses. Furthermore, if you intend to finance the property with a mortgage, you must account for the down payment, which normally ranges between 20% and 25% of the purchase price for an investment property.

For example, if you want to buy a rental property for $250,000, you need be prepared to spend $50,000 to $62,500 ahead for the down payment. Furthermore, closing expenses might range from 2% to 5% of the buying price, increasing your initial investment by $5,000 to $12,500. Being aware of these charges can help you prevent financial stress and ensure that you have enough money to handle all components of the transaction.

Operating expenses are another important aspect of your budget. These include continuing expenses like property taxes, insurance, maintenance and repairs, property management fees, utility bills, and any homeowner association (HOA) fees. It is critical to have a thorough awareness of these expenses in order to effectively forecast your cash flow and ROI.

For example, property taxes might vary greatly based on the location of the property, so it's critical to examine the tax rate in the area where you're investing. Similarly, insurance premiums can vary depending on the age of the property, its location, and the coverage you select. Regular maintenance and repairs are also unavoidable, so allocating a portion of your budget to these costs can keep you from being caught off guard by unexpected charges.

Finally, every sensible investor should have a contingency reserve in their budget. This fund acts as a financial safety net, covering unforeseen expenses such as costly repairs, vacancies, or unexpected declines in rental revenue. Planning for the unexpected allows you to preserve your investment and retain financial security even when things do not go as planned.

Developing a Budget That Aligns With Your Investment Goals

Your budget should be geared to your individual investing goals, whether they are to generate immediate cash flow, develop long-term wealth, or both. This necessitates a thorough understanding of your financial goals and how they influence your budgeting strategy.

Investors looking for immediate cash flow should prioritize assets with high rental revenue potential. In this instance, your budget should prioritize properties in high-demand rental markets, where you may charge higher rents. To achieve regular occupancy and avoid vacancies, consider allocating more cash to marketing and tenant retention.

For example, if your aim is to generate $500 in monthly cash flow from each property, you must budget accordingly. This could include choosing homes in appealing districts, providing amenities that attract tenants, and setting competitive but profitable rent costs. In addition, you'll need to carefully control operating expenses to keep your cash flow positive.

On the other hand, if your major goal is long-term wealth accumulation, you may choose assets with high appreciation potential, even if the immediate income flow is minimal. In this circumstance, your budget may devote more dollars to properties in emerging locations with the potential for significant value appreciation over time. You may also budget for periodic updates and enhancements that will increase the property's value and appeal to potential buyers.

For example, owning a property in a revitalized neighborhood could result in significant long-term returns, even if the initial rental income is smaller than in more established regions. Budgeting for upgrades that coincide with the neighborhood's development will increase the property's worth and position you for future benefits as the area becomes more desired.

Avoiding Common Budget Mistakes

Setting a realistic budget entails more than just crunching numbers; it also entails being aware of frequent blunders that can jeopardize your financial ambitions. One of the most typical blunders is underestimating expenses, especially for maintenance and repairs. Properties, particularly older ones, can necessitate extensive upkeep, and neglecting to budget effectively for these expenses can result in financial distress.

For example, a seemingly small roof repair could turn into a large investment if not addressed quickly. Budgeting for routine inspections and preventative maintenance allows you to avoid costly surprises and keep the property in good shape over time. Setting aside funds for a reserve account expressly for significant, infrequent needs, such as repairing a roof or HVAC system, will also help you stay on track with your budget.

Another typical mistake is to overestimate rental income. It's easy to believe that your home will always be completely occupied and that renters will pay their rent on time each month. However, vacancies, late payments, and tenant turnover are all common aspects of rental property investing. By budgeting cautiously and accounting for potential vacancies or rent decreases, you can keep your financial objectives on track even when rental income varies.

For example, if you anticipate a monthly rental income of $2,000, budget for a slightly lower figure—say, $1,800—to account for potential vacancies or nonpayment. This conservative approach provides a buffer and reduces the chance of financial stress.

Using Tools and Resources for Effective Budgeting

In today's digital age, investors can use a variety of tools and resources to efficiently build and manage rental property budgets. Budgeting software and property management apps can help you track revenue and expenses, estimate cash flow, and alter your budget as needed.

Budgeting applications like Excel, YNAB (You Need a Budget), and property-specific platforms like Stessa or Cozy can assist you in creating precise budgets that include all aspects of your rental property investment. These tools enable you to categorize spending, create financial goals, and generate reports that provide a comprehensive snapshot of your investment's financial performance.

For example, utilizing a property management tool like Cozy can make it easier to collect rent, track expenses, and communicate with tenants—all of which are necessary for remaining within budget. These solutions also include automated reminders for rent payments and maintenance requests, allowing you to manage your properties more efficiently and lowering the chance of financial errors.

Using these tools and resources, you can construct a realistic and adaptive budget, ensuring that you stay on pace to meet your financial objectives.

RESEARCHING AND ANALYSISING THE MARKET

Identifying Promising Locations

When it comes to rental property investing, the location of your investment has a huge impact on your success. Identifying viable locations is a multidimensional process that requires an awareness of economic statistics, community factors, and future growth potential. A well-chosen location not only increases your chances of getting quality tenants, but it also boosts your property's long-term value.

Understanding Economic Indicators

The first step in finding a desirable site is to examine economic statistics that reflect the general health of the market. Key statistics to evaluate include employment rates, median income, and population growth. Areas with strong employment markets often see a continual influx of new people, increasing demand for rental units.

Consider a city with a growing technology sector. As tech businesses expand their operations and hire new staff, the demand for homes in that area is expected to increase. An investor who sees this tendency early may find large chances to purchase rental properties that will generate consistent cash flow and increase in value over time. Austin, Texas, is one example of this, with a surge in technology jobs driving up housing demand and property values.

Evaluation of Neighborhood Characteristics

Beyond larger economic statistics, it's critical to investigate the unique peculiarities of communities in your target area. Even within a same city, neighborhood dynamics can differ drastically. Safety, school quality, and availability to facilities are all important considerations when considering the appeal of an area.

The majority of tenants prioritize safety. Investors should look into crime rates and visit communities at various times to assess safety levels. A community with low crime rates and a reputation for family friendliness is more likely to attract long-term tenants prepared to pay a premium for peace of mind.

The quality of nearby schools might significantly influence the demand for rental houses. Families frequently select regions with high-performing schools, resulting in increased rental interest and potentially higher rents. For example, homes in well-regarded public school districts tend to have lower vacancy rates than those in less desired school districts.

Furthermore, a neighborhood's appeal is heavily influenced by its proximity to amenities such as shopping malls, parks, and public transportation. Tenants value convenience, and a property near bustling shopping districts or efficient transportation choices is more likely to attract decent renters. A classic example is a rental property near a major subway line; tenants may be ready to pay more for convenient access to public transportation that connects them to work centers.

Analysis of Rental Demand and Supply

Understanding supply and demand dynamics in your target location is critical for making sound investment decisions. High demand mixed with limited supply generates a competitive rental market, which raises rental prices. Conversely, oversupply may result in reduced rentals and higher vacancy rates.

A comparative market analysis can provide significant information about rental rates in your target area. Researching similar homes and their rental costs might help you determine whether the investment is in line with your financial objectives. If rental costs are rising in a community, it may signal strong demand, implying that investing there could pay big returns.

For example, if you learn that an area has a high occupancy rate and rental prices have continuously climbed in recent years, this could imply a healthy rental market. Conversely, if there are a lot of "For Rent" signs in the vicinity, it could indicate that the market is oversaturated, and you should reevaluate your investment plan.

Consider Future Development and Growth

Understanding the potential for future growth and development is also an important factor in finding viable places. Areas on the verge of major infrastructural improvements, new commercial ventures, or urban rehabilitation initiatives might provide attractive investment opportunities.

Researching local government plans and zoning revisions might reveal information about neighborhoods that are set for expansion. For example, if a new public transportation route is planned, properties near future stations may experience increasing demand as inhabitants seek more convenient commute options. This foresight can lead to significant increases in property values.

Keep an eye out for developing urban development trends, such as the increase in mixed-use developments that include residential, commercial, and recreational spaces. Investing in communities that embrace this trend can increase the overall appeal of your rental home, attracting tenants who value communal living.

Understanding Local Rules and Zoning Laws

When evaluating potential locations, it's critical to understand local restrictions and zoning laws. These rules can affect your capacity to rent houses and the kind of renters you can attract. Areas with tight zoning rules or rent control measures may limit your earning potential, making them less appealing for investment.

Consulting with local real estate professionals, such as property management firms or real estate attorneys, can provide you with vital information about the local rental market. They can assist you negotiate restrictions and provide advice on how to organize your investments to comply with local laws.

To summarize, evaluating attractive rental property investment areas necessitates a holistic methodology that takes into account economic data, neighborhood characteristics, rental demand, future development possibilities, and local restrictions. By completing thorough research and analysis, you will be able to make informed investment decisions that correspond with your financial goals and position you for success in the rental property market.

Understanding Market Trends

In the ever-changing world of real estate investing, recognizing market trends is like having a compass in new territory. Market trends provide crucial insights that assist investors decide where, when, and how to invest in rental properties. Analyzing these trends allows you to uncover opportunities that correspond with your investment objectives while minimizing the risks associated with market changes.

The Importance Of Economic Cycles

The economic cycle, which includes expansion, peak, contraction, and trough phases, is fundamental to market trends. Recognizing where we are in this cycle can have a huge impact on your investment approach. During an expansion, for example, economic growth leads to greater employment and consumer expenditure. As a result, rental demand tends to increase, making now an excellent time to invest in rental homes.

Consider a community that has lately welcomed a significant employer, such as a technology company. As employment grows, so does the population. This inflow of residents increases demand for housing, resulting in higher rental prices. An astute investor who identifies this tendency can seize the opportunity by purchasing properties in the neighborhood before prices rise further.

In contrast, during a contraction period, economic activity slows and unemployment may increase. During such times, potential tenants may have fewer budgets, resulting in higher vacancy rates and stagnant or dropping rents. Understanding this cycle may cause you to change your investment approach, such as focusing on more cheap properties or waiting new purchases until the market stabilizes.

Demographic Shifts and their Impact

Demographics have an important role in determining rental market trends. Potential tenants' choices and needs vary in tandem with population trends. Age, family size, and lifestyle choices all have a substantial impact on housing demand.

For example, the Millennial age, which has grown to be the largest demographic in many cities, frequently prefers convenience and amenities above traditional homeownership. This tendency has resulted in increased demand for rental apartments in walkable communities near public transportation, restaurants, and entertainment. Investors who target these areas can attract quality tenants willing to pay a premium for lifestyle-oriented property.

Similarly, the aging population is changing the rental market. As Baby Boomers retire and want to downsize or relocate to more manageable living arrangements, demand for single-story houses, retirement communities, and rental properties equipped with accessibility features is likely to increase. Recognizing these demographic patterns might help you select properties that meet the market's shifting needs.

Analysis of Rental Market Metrics

Analyzing important rental market data is essential for gaining a better knowledge of market trends. Vacancy rates, rental price appreciation, and rental yield are all useful variables for determining the health of the rental market.

Vacancy rates, for example, represent the percentage of rental properties that are currently vacant. A low vacancy rate usually indicates high demand, implying that a region may be suitable for investment. In contrast, a high vacancy rate may signal oversupply or falling demand, prompting caution before investing in that location.

Another key measure to keep track of is rental price appreciation. Consistent growth in rental prices over time suggests a robust market that will continue to attract tenants. For example, if an area has had yearly rental price rises of 5% or more in recent years, it indicates that demand is strong and that investing in properties there may offer good returns.

Calculating rental yield, which is the annual income earned by a rental property as a percentage of the purchase price, is critical for determining prospective profitability. A greater rental yield suggests a better investment opportunity, especially in locations where property prices are increasing. For example, if a home costs $200,000 and earns $24,000 in annual rent, its rental yield is 12%. This measure can help you compare investment options and make more educated selections.

Keeping An Eye On Development Projects.

Emerging development projects and infrastructure improvements may potentially indicate prospective changes in market trends. New highways, public transit lines, and commercial areas can have a substantial impact on property values and rental demand. Property prices in an area that has received significant infrastructure investment may climb as accessibility improves, enticing new residents and companies.

For example, if a city announces the development of a new light rail system that will connect previously underserved neighborhoods to the central area, interest in those neighborhoods is likely to increase. Investors anticipate future demand for rental properties in the area, therefore acquiring properties before such projects are completed can result in significant property value gain.

In a similar vein, monitor zoning changes and city planning activities. Areas allocated for future residential or mixed-use developments may experience an increase in demand as they progress. Understanding these elements can help you keep ahead of market trends and effectively place your investments.

Using Technology and Data Analytics

In today's digital age, technology and data analytics are increasingly important in identifying market trends. Rental market data is available in real time through a variety of tools and platforms, including property listing sites, demographic statistics, and economic forecasts.

Data analytics allows you to gain previously unavailable insights into market dynamics. For example, platforms that aggregate data on rental pricing, vacancy rates, and tenant demographics can provide a complete picture of the market. These insights help you make data-driven decisions and improve your investment strategy.

Additionally, social media and internet forums can provide useful insights into tenant preferences and experiences. Engaging with local community groups can help you measure public opinion on specific neighborhoods, possible developments, and housing needs.

Understanding market trends is critical for a successful rental property investment. Analyzing economic cycles, demographic movements, rental market indicators, development initiatives, and using technology can help you find interesting prospects and confidently manage the rental market. This knowledge enables you to make informed investment decisions that are consistent with your financial objectives, ultimately leading to success in wealth creation through rental properties.

Conducting Comparative Market Analysis (CMA).

When navigating the complex world of rental property investing, performing a Comparative Market Analysis (CMA) is a necessary skill that may dramatically improve your decision-making process. A CMA allows you to compare the value of a property to similar properties in the same area, providing valuable information that can help you plan your investment strategy. Whether you're analyzing a new acquisition or setting rental rates for an existing property, a well-executed CMA can be the difference between a wise investment and an expensive error.

Understanding the purpose of a CMA

A Comparative Market Analysis is a tool for determining the fair market value of a property based on recent sales and active listings of comparable properties, also known as "comps." By evaluating these comps, you may determine whether a property is priced correctly and forecast possible rental income. This method is useful for investors seeking to buy, sell, or rent properties because it gives a data-driven foundation for their decisions.

For example, suppose you are thinking about buying a duplex in a suburban community. Conducting a CMA will allow you to locate other duplexes in the neighborhood that have sold within the last six months. This data not only helps you understand the average selling price, but it also provides insights into how rapidly houses sell, which might reflect the strength of demand in that area.

Collecting Data for Your CMA

The first stage in conducting a CMA is acquiring relevant data. This includes data on recently sold properties, active listings, and properties that have expired or been removed from the market. Many real estate websites and platforms provide access to this information, allowing you to compare various property features such as size, location, age, and condition.

When gathering data, look for properties that are comparable to the one you are examining. For example, if you're looking for a three-bedroom, two-bathroom home, your comps should have three bedrooms and two bathrooms, preferably in the same neighborhood. This guarantees that the research includes properties that appeal to a similar group of potential purchasers or renters.

Analyze Comparable Properties

Once you've obtained enough data, the following step is to examine the comparable qualities. Begin by researching the sales prices of recently sold properties. Divide the sale price by the square footage of each comparable property to arrive at the average price per square foot. This amount acts as a baseline for assessing the property you're interested in.

In addition to sale prices, look at the listing prices for existing properties on the market. These prices provide insight into the continuing competition and help you understand other sellers' pricing strategies. For example, if comparable homes are offered at considerably higher prices than your target property, you may need to reconsider your pricing strategy or consider lowering your offer.

Adjusting for differences

Because no two properties are precisely same, you must alter your analysis to account for variances between the subject property and its comparables. Consider lot size, renovations, and location subtleties. If a comparable house has a newly renovated kitchen or is located in a highly sought school district, it may be worth more than your target property.

When making changes, assess the impact of these

disparities. For example, if a comparable sold for $300,000 and had a brand-new roof that would cost you $15,000 to replace, you may reduce the price of your target home by that amount. This method ensures that your value is as precise as possible, which will ultimately guide your investment decisions.

Understanding market conditions

The overall market conditions have a significant impact on your CMA. In a seller's market, where demand exceeds supply, properties may sell for more than the asking price, whereas in a buyer's market, prices may be lower and negotiations more favorable to buyers. Understanding these factors is critical for interpreting your CMA results.

For example, in a seller's market, you may need to change your expectations for the prospective rental income of a property. If similar properties are constantly renting for higher prices owing to rising demand, you may want to adjust your rental rate accordingly to maximize your earnings.

Use CMA for Rental Pricing

In addition to examining purchase prices, a CMA is an effective tool for calculating rental rates. By examining previous rental transactions for comparable properties, you can set a competitive rental rate that attracts qualified tenants while ensuring you meet your financial objectives.

For example, if you own a three-bedroom, two-bathroom single-family house, you would research the rental pricing of comparable homes in your area. If comparable properties rent for $1,800 to $2,000 per month, you can price your property accordingly, accounting for any distinguishing features or additions.

Leveraging Professional Expertise

While a CMA can be completed alone, obtaining the help of a local real estate agent or appraiser can provide significant insights and improve your analysis. These professionals frequently have access to advanced market data and can provide advice on local trends and pricing tactics.

For example, a seasoned real estate agent may give you with knowledge on rising neighborhoods or recent developments, helping you to make informed investment decisions. Their experience and understanding can assist you in avoiding potential hazards and maximizing the value of your investment.

Conducting a comparative market analysis is a critical component of successful rental property investing. You may make better investment decisions by acquiring and analyzing pertinent data, adjusting for property differences, understanding market conditions, and leveraging professional skills. Whether you're evaluating a purchase price or setting rental rates, a well-executed

CMA provides you with the information you need to confidently navigate the real estate market.

FINDING THE RIGHT PROPERTY

Types Of Rental Properties

Understanding the many types of rental properties accessible is critical for making informed decisions that correspond with your financial objectives. Each sort of rental property has its own set of features, perks, and issues. Exploring these possibilities can help you determine which property type is ideal for your investment strategy, risk tolerance, and personal preferences.

Single-Family Homes: A Popular Option

Many new investors prefer single-family houses, and for good reason. These solitary properties, which are built to support one family, are in high demand in residential communities. Single-family houses have the advantage of being easier to finance and manage, especially for first-time investors.

One of the key advantages of investing in single-family houses is the prospect of consistent cash flow. Families looking to rent generally prefer the seclusion and space that these homes offer over apartments or multi-family units. For example, a three-bedroom home in a family-friendly community with strong schools may appeal to long-term tenants who seek a stable living environment. Furthermore, single-family houses frequently increase in value over time, presenting investors with long-term wealth-building opportunities.

However, it is critical to recognize the issues connected with single-family rentals. These properties may have lengthier vacant times between renters, which could affect your cash flow. Furthermore, maintenance expenditures can quickly accumulate, especially if you are responsible for repairs and upkeep.

Multi-Family Properties: Maximising Rental Income

Multi-family homes, such as duplexes, triplexes, and apartment buildings, provide a unique financial opportunity. These homes have several units, so you can earn rental money from multiple renters at the same time. As a result, multifamily properties can generate more cash flow than single-family residences.

For example, investing in a four-unit apartment complex can give you with four different streams of rental income, decreasing the financial impact of vacancies. Even if one unit goes empty, the remaining three continue to generate cash. Furthermore, multi-family properties typically have cheaper maintenance costs per unit because expenses such as landscaping and roof repairs can be shared by tenants.

However, multi-family residences might be more difficult to manage than single-family homes. With several tenants, comes the obligation of managing various lease agreements, tenant complaints, and maintenance requests. Investors should be prepared for the additional time commitment and potential issues that come with managing numerous units.

Low-Maintenance Living In Condominiums And Townhouses

Condominiums and townhouses are another popular rental property type, especially in urban areas. These homes frequently have shared amenities such as pools, exercise centers, and common areas, making them appealing to residents wanting a low-maintenance living. Furthermore, condos and townhouses often require less care than single-family homes, as exterior maintenance is sometimes handled by homeowners' associations (HOAs).

Condos and townhouses may appeal to investors because they have lower purchase prices than single-family homes, especially in high-demand urban regions. For example, a two-bedroom apartment in a desirable location may provide a strong return on investment while needing less initial money than a comparable single-family home.

However, it is necessary to consider the added costs of owning a condo or townhouse. HOAs often charge monthly fees for maintenance and amenities, which might affect your financial flow. Furthermore, the association's rules and regulations may limit your ability to influence property management decisions.

Vacation Rentals: Leveraging Short-Term Demand

Vacation rentals have been increasingly popular in recent years, thanks to companies such as Airbnb and VRBO. These properties cater to travelers looking for short-term accommodations, which are frequently located in tourist areas or urban centers. Investing in vacation rentals can be profitable because they often charge higher nightly rates than standard long-term rentals.

For example, a beach house or mountain cottage can draw guests during peak seasons, making a lot of money in a short period of time. Investors can increase their earnings by proactively marketing their properties and optimizing occupancy rates all year.

However, holiday rentals provide particular obstacles, such as seasonal demand fluctuations, local laws, and the necessity for continual marketing efforts. Investors must be willing to provide hands-on management in order to maintain high visitor satisfaction and keep their properties booked.

Commercial Properties: A Different Type of Investment

While novice investors frequently focus on residential rental properties, commercial properties offer an alternative source of income. Commercial properties include office buildings, retail areas, warehouses, and manufacturing facilities. Commercial leases are typically longer and feature extra income sources, such as percentage rent depending on sales, which can result in larger returns on investment.

For example, investing in retail space leased to a well-known brand can give a consistent revenue stream over time while simultaneously benefiting from property appreciation. However, commercial buildings provide distinct issues, such as greater borrowing costs, increased economic sensitivity, and more complex leasing agreements.

Furthermore, commercial real estate may necessitate a more in-depth grasp of market dynamics and tenant needs, making it critical for investors to perform extensive study and analysis before entering this area.

The Right Fit for You.

Finally, the best form of rental property relies on your investment objectives, financial circumstances, and personal preferences. Consider your intended level of involvement, risk tolerance, and available time for property management.

For example, if you want a hands-off approach, investing in single-family houses or condominiums with reputable property management could be suitable. A multi-family property or vacation rental, on the other hand, may be the ideal choice if you prefer managing several tenants and maximizing income flow.

By researching the many types of rental properties

accessible, you can make informed decisions that are consistent with your investment plan and will help you reach your financial objectives in the world of rental property investing.

Working with Real Estate Agents

Navigating the world of rental property investing may be difficult, particularly for beginners. With so many properties on the market and so many aspects to consider, hiring a professional real estate agent can be a huge assistance. A qualified realtor not only brings experience to the table, but also a network of resources and insights that can greatly help you with your property search. Understanding how to communicate effectively with a real estate agent is critical for making sound investing decisions.

The value of expertise

Real estate brokers have specific knowledge of the local market, which can provide you a competitive advantage. They have access to property price statistics, neighborhood patterns, and other vital information that the average investor may not have. For example, an agent who is knowledgeable with a certain location can direct you to communities that are growing or developing, allowing you to locate prospective investment prospects.

Furthermore, agents are educated to spot potential red flags in properties that would otherwise go unnoticed.

They can identify issues such as structural flaws, zoning restrictions, or evidence of neglect that could jeopardize your investment. By harnessing their experience, you can prevent costly mistakes and make wise investments.

Finding The Right Agent

Selecting the correct real estate agent is critical to a successful partnership. Look for agents who specialize in investment homes and have a strong reputation in the local market. Consider their background, client testimonials, and whether they understand your investment objectives. For example, if you are interested in multi-family properties, look for an agent that has already assisted other investors in the region.

Once you've discovered possible agents, conduct interviews to determine their suitability. Inquire about their experience working with investors, their understanding of the local market, and their approach to property searches. A excellent agent will take the time to understand your goals and be willing to modify their techniques to match your requirements.

Setting Clear Expectations

Setting clear expectations from the start is critical to a good working relationship with your agent. Discuss your rental budget, preferred property types, and desired characteristics. By outlining your investing requirements, your agent can personalize their search to meet your objectives.

For example, if you want to find a single-family house in a family-friendly community close to schools and parks, inform your realtor. This clarity allows them to focus their search and offer you with properties that match your preferences. Establish communication preferences, such as how frequently you want to receive information on new postings and your preferred means of communication.

Leveraging Market Knowledge

One of the most significant benefits of dealing with a real estate agent is their extensive knowledge of market trends. Agents are continually monitoring changes in the local market, such as pricing, inventory levels, and growing areas. This information can help with your home search.

For example, if an area sees an influx of new enterprises or infrastructural development, property values may grow in the near future. Your agent may point out such tendencies and assist you discover properties that may appreciate greatly over time. You may make better financial selections by harnessing your market expertise.

Access to Off-Market Listings

In addition to listed homes, real estate agents frequently have access to off-market offerings that are not widely promoted. These homes can be hidden treasures, providing chances that other investors may miss. An experienced agent may have connections with other agents, investors, or property owners who are thinking about selling but have not yet posted their properties.

For example, if your realtor learns about a landlord who wants to sell a rental property before it reaches the market, you may be able to make an offer before the competition heats up. This can provide you a major advantage in a competitive market, allowing you to purchase a property at a lower price.

How to Navigate Negotiations and Transactions

Real estate transactions can be complicated, but having an experienced agent on your side can help ease the process. Agents are excellent negotiators who understand how to speak for your best interests, whether you're making an offer on a home or negotiating repairs following a home inspection.

For example, if you discover difficulties during a property inspection, your agent can work with the seller to either fix the problems before closing or present you with a credit at closing to cover the necessary repairs. This knowledge can help you save money and ensure that your investment is safe.

In addition, agents are aware with the paperwork and legal requirements associated with real estate transactions. They can walk you through the essential paperwork, ensuring that everything is done correctly and on schedule. This assistance can relieve some of the stress involved with property transfers, allowing you to concentrate on your investing objectives.

Forming a Long-Term Partnership

Working with a real estate agent can result in a long-term partnership that benefits your investing journey. A qualified agent will continue to offer assistance and advice as your investment portfolio increases. They can help you find more homes, advise on market changes, and connect with property management companies.

Consider building a good relationship with your agent by staying in touch after your initial purchase. Share your future financial goals with them, and seek their guidance as you explore new alternatives. This ongoing cooperation can give you with the resources and insights you need to succeed in rental property investing over the long run.

In conclusion, working with an experienced real estate agent is an important step in your path as a rental property investor. Their experience, market knowledge, and negotiation abilities can help you improve your property search and make more educated decisions. By hiring the proper agent and setting clear expectations, you may confidently navigate the complex world of real estate, ultimately leading to successful investments that meet your financial objectives.

Evaluating Potential Properties

In the world of rental property investing, evaluating possible properties is a critical stage that can have a big impact on your long-term performance. While the temptation of a good listing is appealing, taking a methodical approach to examining each property ensures that you make informed judgments that are consistent with your investment objectives. This procedure entails evaluating several characteristics of a property, including its condition, location, potential cash flow, and general market landscape.

Understanding Property Conditions

The physical condition of a property is critical to establishing its feasibility as a rental investment. Before making any decisions, a comprehensive inspection is required. This inspection should include both the inside and the exterior, with a focus on critical components including the roof, foundation, plumbing, electrical systems, and HVAC. For example, a roof that is nearing the end of its useful life may necessitate costly repairs or replacement shortly after purchase, affecting your cash flow.

It's a good idea to take extensive notes and images of any problems found during the examination. These documents can be used as the basis for discussions with the seller. If extensive repairs are required, you can request that they be completed before closing or negotiate a price decrease to cover future expenses.

Hiring a trained house inspector can also provide significant insights that go beyond the outward symptoms of wear and tear, allowing you to avoid potential traps.

Evaluation of Location and Neighborhood Dynamics

The location of a property is frequently the most important aspect in determining its long-term value and rental potential. A good neighborhood can attract great tenants and generate consistent rental income, but a less favorable location may struggle to sustain occupancy rates. When analyzing potential properties, keep schools, retail malls, public transportation, and job prospects in mind.

For example, a property within walking distance of a well-known school district may appeal to families, resulting in lower vacancy rates and longer lease durations. Similarly, houses near large employers or public transportation routes may attract young professionals who appreciate convenience. Researching area demographics and patterns can also help predict future growth or decline. Are there any evidence of new construction in the area? Is there a demand for rentals as the population grows? These elements can have a long-term impact on the success of your venture.

Analysis of Potential Cash Flow

A comprehensive analysis of a property's potential cash flow is required to determine its financial sustainability as a rental investment. Begin by evaluating the projected rental revenue using comparable homes in the region. Look for similar units that have recently been rented and utilize this information to predict reasonable rental prices for your desired home.

Once you've estimated your rental revenue, figure up your running expenses, which may include property management fees, property taxes, insurance, maintenance costs, and utilities. For example, if your expected rental revenue is $1,500 per month and your total monthly expenses are $1,000, your cash flow before mortgage payments will be $500.

After calculating your operating expenses, include your mortgage payment to get a comprehensive picture of your overall cash flow. If your mortgage payment is $800, your net cash flow is $500 minus $800 = -$300. This negative cash flow could suggest that the property is not financially viable without changes to rental pricing or spending control. Aiming for positive cash flow is critical for covering unforeseen expenses and increasing equity in your investment.

Consider Market Comparisons

Conducting a comparative market analysis (CMA) is an important stage in assessing potential assets. This method entails examining recently sold and rented properties in the neighborhood to acquire insight into market patterns and property values. Looking at similar homes allows you to decide whether a listing is adequately priced and understand the elements driving local demand.

For example, if you're looking at a multi-family home that is much more expensive than comparable units with similar square footage and amenities, it may be time to haggle or seek elsewhere. On the other side, if you discover a property priced lower than comparable listings, it may provide a chance for value appreciation or increased cash flow.

Furthermore, checking the days on market for comparable properties might provide information about local demand. If properties sell or rent rapidly, it may signal a competitive market, which could lead to higher rental rates. In contrast, properties that remain on the market may indicate oversupply or diminishing demand, necessitating more study into the causes.

Measuring Future Growth Potential

When analyzing potential properties, think about the area's long-term growth potential. Economic development, infrastructure initiatives, and demographic shifts all have an impact on property values and rental demand. Investigate local growth and development plans, such as new enterprises in the neighborhood, public transit expansions, or large road building projects.

For example, if a city announces plans for a new innovation hub or business park, properties in the surrounding area may find increased demand as new employees seek residence. Understanding these dynamics will allow you to make more informed investing decisions and position yourself for future growth.

Understanding Local Rules and Zoning Laws

Finally, educate yourself with local regulations and zoning laws that may apply to your rental property. Each municipality has its own set of rules for rental homes, which include licensing requirements, property upkeep standards, and tenant rights. These restrictions might vary greatly, so it is critical to research the specific requirements in the region where you intend to invest.

Some cities, for example, prohibit short-term rentals, while others require landlords to follow specified building requirements or tenant screening procedures. Understanding these requirements might help you avoid legal complications and ensure that your investment is in accordance with local laws.

By taking a holistic approach to evaluating possible properties, you may make informed judgments that are consistent with your financial objectives. Understanding the property's condition and location dynamics, as well as analyzing cash flow prospects and market trends, are all important aspects of your investment journey. Armed with the necessary information and insights, you'll be better able to select a rental property that not only matches your financial goals but also puts you on track for success in the world of rental property investing.

OBTAINING FINANCING FOR YOUR INVESTMENT

Understanding Financing Options

Securing the right finance is a critical stage in the rental property investment process. With so many options available, recognizing their subtleties can help you make informed selections that correspond with your financial goals. Whether you are a first-time investor or want to diversify your portfolio, understanding the financing landscape takes a deliberate strategy. Let's look at the different financing choices available, their merits and downsides, and how they can affect your investing path.

Conventional mortgages

A conventional mortgage is one of the most prevalent financing options for rental properties. Banks and credit unions often issue these loans, which demand a solid credit score, a consistent income, and a 20% down payment for investment properties. The fundamental appeal of traditional mortgages is their simplicity; they come with fixed or adjustable interest rates and clear payback conditions.

For example, a fixed-rate mortgage allows you to lock in a set interest rate for the duration of the loan, ensuring that your monthly payments are predictable. This steadiness can be very useful for forecasting cash flow for rental properties. Adjustable-rate mortgages (ARMs) may start with lower interest rates, resulting in lower beginning payments. However, these rates can fluctuate, creating uncertainty in future payments.

FHA Loans for Multifamily Properties

If you're thinking about investing in multi-unit homes, Federal Housing Administration (FHA) loans may be a good option. FHA loans are intended to assist low- to moderate-income purchasers in purchasing houses with reduced down payments—typically as low as 3.5%. These loans can also be used for homes with up to four apartments, as long as the owner lives in one of them.

This financing method allows investors to enter into rental properties with a low initial investment. For example, if you buy a fourplex for $400,000, a 3.5% down payment is only $14,000. This can be an excellent option for new investors to create wealth while living in one unit and renting out the rest to offset mortgage bills. However, it is critical to understand the obligation to live in one of the units, which may not suit every investor's objectives.

Portfolio loans

Portfolio loans can be a great option for experienced investors or those wishing to buy many homes. Unlike typical loans, which are sold to investors on the secondary market, portfolio loans are held in-house by the lending institution. This means that lenders have greater flexibility in their underwriting standards and can accommodate unique situations.

Portfolio loans are commonly employed by investors who have a large number of current loans or who own properties that do not fit the severe requirements of traditional finance. For example, if an investor owns many properties and wishes to purchase another, a lender offering portfolio loans may be more inclined to consider the whole revenue provided by the investor's portfolio rather than just one property's cash flow.

Hard Cash Loans

Hard money loans are short-term, high-interest loans backed by real estate. These loans are commonly employed by investors in need of quick funding, particularly for fix-and-flip projects or homes that require extensive improvements. Because hard money lenders prioritize the property's value over the borrower's creditworthiness, these loans can be closed faster than standard finance.

For example, if you come across a distressed home that you believe can be flipped for a profit, a hard money loan could offer the finances needed to buy and rehabilitate it. However, these loans have higher interest rates and shorter repayment durations, so it's critical to have a good exit strategy in place before choosing this financing option.

Private Money Loans

Private money loans are another alternative for rental

property investors, which are frequently obtained from people or groups rather than established banking institutions. These loans might have more flexible terms and conditions, making them an appealing choice for investors looking for non-traditional funding.

For example, if you have a network of friends or family members who want to invest in your home, you may draw out a private loan agreement that benefits both sides. Private money lenders typically provide speedier access to loans and may not require as much documentation as traditional lenders. However, it is critical to establish the terms in writing to minimize future misunderstandings.

Home equity loans and lines of credit

If you already own a home or an investment property with sufficient value, you may want to explore using home equity loans or lines of credit (HELOCs). A home equity loan allows you to borrow a single sum against the equity in your home, whereas a HELOC is more like a credit card, offering a revolving line of credit based on the value of your property.

For example, if your property is worth $300,000 and you owe $200,000 on your mortgage, you could have $100,000 in equity. A lender may allow you to borrow a portion of your equity to fund your rental property acquisition or upgrades. This can be a cost-effective approach to fund your assets, especially if you get a lower interest rate than other financing options.

Crowdfunding

As the real estate market advances, crowdfunding has emerged as an attractive financing option for investors. Real estate crowdfunding platforms enable several investors to pool their funds to finance a property purchase or development project. This can be an appealing choice for those who do not have the funds to invest individually in a rental property.

For example, if a property is listed at $1 million, a crowdfunding site may allow ten investors to each contribute $100,000. This collaborative strategy may allow individual investors to have access to larger ventures that would otherwise be out of reach. However, before investing funds, undertake extensive due diligence on the crowdfunding platform and the specific investment opportunity.

Navigating Financing Challenges

Understanding your financial alternatives is critical, but so is being aware of potential obstacles. Lenders often look at borrowers' credit histories, income levels, and debt-to-income ratios when reviewing loan applications. Maintaining a strong credit score and controlling existing debt are critical for investors seeking advantageous financing arrangements.

Also, be prepared for any market volatility that may affect interest rates or loan criteria. Economic developments may impact your capacity to obtain funding, so having a backup plan or alternate financing sources in place will provide piece of mind.

The Importance Of Financial Planning

Finally, comprehensive financial preparation is essential for successfully navigating the funding landscape. Consider your long-term investing objectives, your existing financial condition, and the impact of each financing option on your overall strategy. Consider speaking with a financial counselor or mortgage broker that specializes in investment properties to get advice suited to your specific situation.

You may confidently pursue your rental property investing ambitions if you are well-versed in your financing alternatives and address potential obstacles ahead of time. Understanding the nuances of each option allows you to make informed judgments that will pave the way for your success in the world of real estate investing.

Preparing Your Financial Documents

Securing funding for your rental property is a crucial step that demands meticulous planning and attention to detail. Lenders must analyze your financial stability and estimate the risk associated with lending to you. This is where your financial records come into play. They provide a thorough picture of your financial situation, demonstrating your ability to manage debt and successfully produce revenue from your investments. Preparing these documents thoroughly might speed up the approval process and boost your chances of obtaining the best loan alternatives available.

Understanding Essential Financial Documents

When approaching a lender, you will normally be requested for a variety of financial documentation. These records contain information about your income, assets, and overall financial condition. Frequently requested goods include:

- **Tax Returns:** Lenders frequently request the last two years' personal and corporate tax returns. This gives them an accurate picture of your earning history and financial stability. It's critical that these paperwork are comprehensive, correct, and reflect your actual earnings. For example, if you are self-employed, your tax returns should show your revenue streams and any deductible expenses, as this may influence how lenders evaluate your financial stability.

- **Pay Stubs and W-2s:** If you are employed, your lender will most likely require current pay stubs and W-2 forms. These documents help to verify your employment status and income level. If you receive bonuses or commissions, it is helpful to offer additional paperwork to show how these items affect your entire revenue.

- **Bank Statements:** Lenders will want to analyze your bank statements from the last two to three months. These statements are proof of your financial practices, demonstrating your capacity to save and manage money. It is critical to ensure that your records reflect enough reserves, as lenders frequently seek for evidence of cash reserves that can cover mortgage payments in the event of vacancy or unforeseen expenses.

- **Asset Statements:** Documenting your assets is essential for establishing your financial strength. This can contain statements for investment accounts, retirement accounts, and other significant assets like real estate or vehicles. By exhibiting your assets, you reassure lenders that you have the resources to back up your investment.

Organize Your Financial Documents

Once you've identified the papers you need, the next step is to efficiently organize them. Creating a digital or physical file dedicated to your financial data will help streamline the process and guarantee you have all you need when asking for funding. Here are some tips for an efficient organization:

- **Label and Date Documents:** Clearly label each document with the date it was issued. This allows lenders to swiftly determine the relevancy and currency of the material. For example, instead of simply stating "bank statement," name it "Chase Bank Savings Account Statement - January 2024."

- **Create a Checklist:** As you gather your documents,

make a checklist to keep track of what you have and what you still need. This will allow you to keep organized and avoid last-minute scrambles for missing documentation.

- Review for Accuracy: Before submitting your documents, thoroughly check them for accuracy. Small inaccuracies can raise red flags for lenders, so make sure your income statistics, account balances, and other key information are precise.

- Use Professional Formatting: When submitting documents such as company plans or financial statements, consider utilizing professional formatting. A polished presentation not only displays professionalism, but also makes it easier for lenders to understand the material.

Understanding your credit report

In addition to financial papers, lenders will review your credit report to determine your creditworthiness. A good credit score can have a big impact on your ability to obtain financing and the terms you are offered. Before approaching lenders, request a copy of your credit report and check it for any errors or places for improvement. Here are some steps to take with your credit report:

- Check for Errors: Errors on your credit report might lower your score. Check for any errors, such as erroneous account information or out-of-date debts. If you uncover any differences, take the proper measures to dispute them with the credit bureau.

- Understand Your Credit Score: Familiarize yourself with the different components of your credit score. Payment history, credit use, and credit history length are all important factors to consider. Understanding these components will help you discover areas for improvement before applying for finance.

- Boosting Your Credit Score: If your credit score is lower than you would like, consider taking actions to enhance it before applying for loans. This could include paying off credit card balances, making all payments on time, and abstaining from acquiring new lines of credit in the months preceding your application.

Getting Ready For Questions And Explanations

When presenting your financial documentation to lenders, be prepared to answer inquiries and explain your financial history. For example, if your income or expenses fluctuate significantly, being transparent and providing context might help reduce anxieties. Consider the following.

- Create a Narrative: Prepare to share your financial experience, including any obstacles you've encountered and how you overcame them. This narrative might assist lenders comprehend your financial situation and your dedication to responsible investment management.

- Highlight Future Potential: If you're switching to

rental property investing, underline your goals to make money from these properties. Discuss your research, awareness of market trends, and anticipated future cash flow, demonstrating your readiness and dedication.

- Interact with Your Lender: Build a rapport with your lender by being open and conversational. A positive relationship can result in better terms and support during the approval process.

Preparing your financial documentation is an important step in obtaining funding for your rental property investment. Understanding what lenders demand, correctly arranging your records, and being proactive about your credit profile will set you up for success. This preparedness not only gives lenders confidence, but also enables you to navigate the financing landscape with clarity and assurance, laying the groundwork for a successful investment journey.

Getting Pre-Approved for a Loan

Securing a financing for your rental property is an important stage in the investment process, and getting pre-approval is often the first step. Pre-approval not only allows you to better understand your budget, but it also establishes you as a serious buyer in a competitive market. Before making an offer, lenders evaluate your creditworthiness, income, and general financial health to provide you with a concrete loan amount with which you can work confidently.

What is the difference between pre-approval and pre-qualification?

Before beginning the pre-approval process, it's important to distinguish between pre-approval and pre-qualification, as these terms are sometimes used interchangeably but have different meanings.

Pre-qualification is often a less formal assessment based on self-reported financial information. You enter basic information about your income, assets, and debts, and the lender estimates how much you could borrow. While pre-qualification might help you get a basic understanding of your budget, it does not need a credit check, thus it has less weight in the eyes of sellers.

Pre-approval, on the other hand, is a more official process. It entails providing thorough financial information and undertaking a credit check. Lenders conduct a more thorough assessment of your financial status before approving you for a specific loan amount. This not only clarifies your budget, but also communicates to vendors that you are a serious buyer. In competitive markets, having a pre-approval letter can mean the difference between getting your dream home or losing it to another buyer.

The Pre-approval Process

Getting pre-approved is a simple procedure, but it does require some preparation. Here's how to successfully navigate it:

Collecting Financial Documents

To begin, acquire the necessary financial documentation that lenders will require for a thorough examination. Common documents include:

- **Recent pay stubs or evidence of income:** This confirms your work status and demonstrates to lenders that you have a consistent source of income to support mortgage payments.

- **Tax returns from the past two years:** These documents provide information about your wages and financial stability by displaying your income sources and general financial picture.

- **Bank statements:** Lenders frequently require bank statements to determine your cash reserves and spending habits. A healthy savings account can demonstrate your ability to cover unforeseen bills or vacancies in your rental property.

- **Asset documentation:** Keep track of any investments, retirement accounts, or other important assets that can help your financial situation.

Having these documents structured and easily available helps speed up the pre-approval process, allowing lenders to examine your circumstances swiftly.

Submit Your Application

Once your financial documents are in order, you can apply for pre-approval. Most lenders have online applications that will take you through the procedure. Prepare to supply personal information such as your Social Security number, work data, and any outstanding debts.

During this phase, your credit will be checked, which will have a temporary impact on your score. However, it is vital for lenders to assess your creditworthiness. After you submit your application, the lender will look over your financial information, credit history, and the papers you provided.

Receiving your pre-approval letter

Following a successful evaluation, the lender will issue a pre-approval letter outlining the maximum loan amount you can obtain. This letter typically contains:

- **The loan amount:** This is the maximum amount you are pre-approved to borrow, which can help you set a budget when looking for properties.

- **The loan terms:** The pre-approval letter specifies the loan type, interest rate, and any other terms that may apply. Understanding these phrases enables you to compare various financial choices.

- **The validity period:** Pre-approval letters frequently

include an expiration date, which ranges from 60 to 90 days. This implies you should actively look for properties within this time span to make the most of your pre-approval.

Creating a Strong Case for Pre-approval

To increase your chances of obtaining pre-approval, consider the following suggestions:

- Improve Your Credit Score: Before applying, check your credit record for errors and correct them. If your credit score is low, try taking efforts to enhance it, such as paying off existing obligations or making on-time payments.

- Boost Your Income or Cash Reserves: If possible, improve your financial situation by increasing your income or saving more money. This increases your chances of being pre-approved and may possibly qualify you for better loan conditions.

- Avoid Major Financial Changes: Lenders value stability. If you intend to make big financial changes, such as changing jobs or taking on additional debt, consider deferring them until you obtain pre-approval.

Use Your Pre-Approval

Once you have received your pre-approval letter, you may begin your property search with confidence. With your pre-approval, you'll have a set budget and the option to make offers on houses. Sellers are more likely to take your offers seriously if you have been pre-approved, making you a more appealing bidder.

Furthermore, obtaining a pre-approval can provide you an advantage in negotiations. If you locate a property you want, you can act swiftly to show sellers that you are ready and serious about your investment. This can be especially useful in a competitive market where homes may receive many offers.

CONDUCTING DUE DILIGENCE

Property Inspections and Appraisals

When considering purchasing a rental property, careful due diligence is an important step that can protect your investment. Property inspections and appraisals not only provide useful information about the property's condition, but they also assist you make informed financial decisions. Skipping this critical step can result in unexpected expenditures and hassles that may jeopardize your investing intentions.

The Importance of Property Inspection

A property inspection acts as your eyes and ears throughout the purchasing process. It is a thorough physical evaluation of the property undertaken by a skilled home inspector. The inspector will analyze the property's structural integrity, systems (such as plumbing and electrical), and general environmental safety.

Understanding the value of property inspections extends beyond simply confirming the property's condition; it also allows you to identify potential issues that may affect your return on investment. For example, if the inspector finds roof damage or plumbing problems, you may have to negotiate repairs with the seller or reconsider your purchase entirely.

What to Expect during a Property Inspection

During a property inspection, the inspector will thoroughly examine both the inside and outside of the home. This involves assessing:

- **Foundation and Structure:** Inspectors will search for cracks, settling, and evidence of structural deterioration. A solid foundation is required to ensure the property's long-term integrity.

- **Roof and Gutters:** The quality of your roof might significantly affect your future costs. Inspectors will look for leaks, missing shingles, and the general longevity of the roof.

- **HVAC Systems:** Proper heating and cooling systems are critical to tenant comfort and energy efficiency. Inspectors will assess the condition and functionality of the heating, ventilation, and air conditioning systems.

- **Plumbing and Electrical Systems:** Inspectors will inspect the plumbing for leaks and water pressure issues, as well as the electrical systems for safety and code compliance. Faulty plumbing or electrical can endanger residents and demand costly repairs.

Following the inspection, you will receive a thorough report explaining any faults discovered, as well as recommendations for repairs or more examination. This report is an essential tool for negotiating with the seller or making an informed decision to proceed with the acquisition.

Interact with Inspectors and Their Findings

As a buyer, you should interact with the inspector throughout the home inspection. Accompanying them helps you to ask questions, clarify results, and acquire a better idea of the property's condition. For example, if the inspector points out a minor fault, you can query about possible solutions and associated expenses.

Furthermore, taking a proactive approach might help you establish relationship with the inspector, who may provide insights beyond the report. Their experience can provide crucial insight into whether certain concerns are typical in the area or should be handled seriously.

Understanding Appraisals

An assessment determines the property's fair market value, whereas a property inspection assesses its physical condition. Lenders frequently require licensed appraisers to make appraisals before to approving a mortgage. The appraiser evaluates the property by examining a number of characteristics, including:

- **Comparable Sales:** The appraiser will look at recent sales of comparable homes in the area, known as "comps." This research helps to determine a reasonable market value based on current market conditions.

- **Property Condition:** The appraiser will assess the

property's condition, layout, and any upgrades or repairs that have been completed. Well-maintained properties often value better than those that require considerable repairs.

- Location and community: The appraiser evaluates the property's location, which includes its closeness to amenities, schools, public transportation, and general community appeal. These factors can have a substantial impact on property values.

How To Prepare for an Appraisal

To prepare for an appraisal, make sure the property is tidy and well-kept. Making simple upgrades, such as landscaping or new paint, might boost the property's attractiveness. Furthermore, giving the appraiser with a list of recent updates, repairs, and area features might assist them justify your asking price.

It's also critical to understand the evaluated worth and how it influences your investment plan. If the appraisal is lower than expected, you may need to negotiate a reduced purchase price or consider walking away from the transaction. In contrast, a higher assessment might serve as a solid foundation for your investment, confirming that you made the right decision.

How to Use Inspection and Appraisal Results to Your Advantage

When you obtain the inspection and assessment reports,

use the knowledge strategically. If the inspection shows severe flaws, try negotiating with the seller for repairs or a lower purchase price. This negotiation has the potential to save you a lot of money over time.

Additionally, if the appraisal supports your purchase price, you can proceed with confidence. A positive appraisal validates your investment decision and assures that your financial outlay is consistent with market values.

Property inspections and appraisals are more than just a formality; they are an important part of the due diligence process. Understanding what to expect and how to apply these findings enables you to make informed decisions, bargain successfully, and ultimately protect your investment in the rental property market.

Assessing Legal and Zoning Concerns

Navigating the legal landscape is a critical stage in the process of purchasing rental property. Understanding the legal and zoning concerns that may effect your investment can allow you to prevent costly mistakes and guarantee that your property complies with local standards. This chapter digs into the key parts of assessing legal and zoning difficulties, providing you with the knowledge you need to make sound property investment decisions.

Understanding Zoning Laws

Zoning rules are local regulations that govern how property in a given region can be used. These regulations govern what types of structures can be built, how properties can be used, and the density of growth in a specific area. Understanding zoning classifications is critical for property investors since it has a direct impact on a property's prospective uses and any future modifications.

Residential zoning, for example, permits single-family homes, apartments, or townhouses, whereas commercial zoning allows for retail stores, offices, or service firms. Furthermore, some locations may have mixed-use zoning, which combines residential and business components. Familiarizing yourself with the zoning restrictions in your desired area will assist you avoid buying properties that do not match your investment goals.

Examining Property-Specific Zoning Regulations

Before buying a property, it is critical to research the exact zoning regulations that apply to it. This research is often conducted through the local zoning office or municipal planning department, where you can obtain property records and zoning maps. Key questions to address while conducting research include:

- What is the current zoning classification for the property?

- Has the current owner secured any zoning variances or special permits?
- Are there any restrictions on property changes, such as setbacks, height limits, or lot coverage?

For example, if you want to convert a single-family home into a multi-unit rental, you must first understand the zoning regulations and any necessary deviations. Failure to follow zoning restrictions may result in fines, mandated changes, or even forced property removal.

Understanding local laws and regulations

Aside from zoning restrictions, there are a number of municipal regulations that can affect your rental property investment. These regulations may address a variety of issues, such as tenant rights, rental agreements, and property maintenance standards. Familiarizing yourself with these regulations guarantees that you stay within legal limits and protects you from potential legal action.

For example, some towns have rent control regulations that limit how much landlords may charge for rent hikes. Understanding these laws enables you to establish realistic financial goals for your investment. Additionally, become acquainted with local landlord-tenant laws, which frequently specify how security deposits must be handled, the notice periods required for evictions, and the procedures for dealing with tenant complaints.

Assessing Property Liens And Encumbrances

Another important part of due diligence is determining whether there are any liens or encumbrances on the property. A lien is a legal claim against property that arises from unpaid payments, such as property taxes or contractor bills. An encumbrance, on the other hand, may contain easements or limitations that limit how the property can be used.

Before finalizing your acquisition, you should do a title search to find any existing liens or encumbrances. This step usually include dealing with a title firm or a real estate attorney to help unearth any hidden concerns. Understanding these elements is critical since they can impact your property ownership and financial returns.

For example, if you buy a home with an ongoing tax lien, you may inherit the debt, affecting your cash flow and investing strategy. Similarly, an easement that permits a neighbor to use a section of your property may restrict your freedom to develop or change the area as you like.

Role of Professional Assistance

Given the complexities of legal and zoning concerns, working with professionals can greatly improve your due diligence process. Real estate attorneys can provide vital information about local regulations, assist with title searches, and interpret zoning laws. Working with skilled professionals can assist you in avoiding potential hazards and ensuring compliance with all applicable legal obligations.

Furthermore, engaging the assistance of local real estate brokers who are familiar with the market may provide you with information on which neighborhoods are seeing growth, the types of homes in demand, and prospective zoning changes on the horizon. Their experience can help you gain a better understanding of the risks and opportunities connected with various investments.

Evaluation of Future Zoning Changes

Finally, evaluate the possibility of future zoning changes in the region you're interested in. Local governments examine and amend zoning ordinances on a regular basis to reflect population growth, community needs, and development trends. Staying updated about forthcoming changes can provide you a competitive advantage and help you predict how new regulations will affect your investment.

For example, if a neighborhood is being revitalized and commercial development is planned, property values and rental demand may grow. In contrast, zoning a region for high-density housing may raise competition for your rental property.

Assessing legal and zoning difficulties is an important part of the due diligence process when investing in rental properties. Understanding zoning laws, examining property-specific rules, and evaluating liens and encumbrances will protect your investment and position you for long-term success in the real estate market. Engaging with professionals and staying current on future zoning changes will help you negotiate the complexity of property investment. With a proactive approach to legal and zoning matters, you'll be well-positioned to establish a profitable rental property portfolio.

Calculating Renovations And Repair Costs

When investing in rental properties, the possibility of renovations and repairs is frequently a reality that ambitious landlords must confront. Understanding how to appropriately calculate these costs is critical since it influences your overall investment plan, cash flow, and return on investment (ROI). By carefully estimating renovation and repair costs, you may make informed decisions that increase the property's worth while being financially viable.

The Importance of Accurate Cost Estimate

Accurate cost estimation is more than simply a best practice; it is essential for successful property investing. Overestimating renovation expenses can lead to wasteful spending, whereas underestimating can result in budget overruns that jeopardize your profitability. As a result, taking a systematic approach to assessing these expenditures will help you create realistic budgets and prevent financial mistakes.

Understanding The Many Types Of Renovation Costs

When evaluating renovation and repair expenditures, it's important to distinguish between the various sorts of charges that may arise. These can be broadly classified into several important areas:

1. Cosmetic Improvements: These are surface-level improvements intended to improve the property's visual appeal without affecting its structure. Examples include painting walls, installing new flooring, and replacing light fixtures. While these adjustments can considerably improve the property's marketability, they are typically less expensive than structural renovations.

2. Structural Repairs: These are changes that affect the structure or layout of the property. Structural repairs can range from repairing a broken foundation to replacing the roof. These projects are often more expensive, necessitating careful planning and contractor control.

3. System Upgrades: Older homes may require improvements to critical systems like plumbing, electrical, or HVAC (heating, ventilation, and air conditioning). Upgrading these systems is not only necessary for tenant safety and comfort, but it can also help to avoid costly future repairs.

4. Landscaping and Exterior Work: The exterior of a property contributes significantly to curb appeal, which can affect a prospective tenant's decision to rent. Planting new trees, laying grass, or paving walkways are

all examples of landscaping costs, and while these enhancements might improve aesthetics, they can increase overall costs.

Conducting Comprehensive Cost Analysis

To build an appropriate budget for renovation and repair costs, take a systematic approach. Begin by examining the property's existing state and identifying areas that require renovation. Use the inspection report to guide your study, then prioritize repairs based on urgency and potential impact on rental income.

Once you've determined the necessary modifications, you may estimate the expenses for each job. For example, if you intend to rebuild a kitchen, consider the following expenses:

- **Labor Costs:** Hiring contractors for expert labor might consume a large percentage of your money. Collect quotes from several contractors to guarantee you are getting fair pricing.

- **Materials:** The price of materials varies greatly based on quality and variety. To identify the greatest fit for your investment goals, compare several suppliers and materials, ranging from low-cost alternatives to high-end finishes.

- **Permits and Inspections:** Depending on the extent of your project, you may require permits or inspections. Be sure to account for these expenditures, as they are commonly omitted in initial calculations.

Using Cost Estimation Tools and Resources

Many tools and services can help you estimate renovation and repair costs more accurately. Online calculators can provide preliminary estimates based on industry norms, while contractor-specific apps allow you to track expenditures in real time.

Networking with local contractors and experienced investors can help provide insight into the costs of various sorts of projects. Consider joining local real estate investor events or forums where you can share information and acquire valuable insights from others who have been through similar experiences.

The Importance of Contingency Budgets

Even with careful planning and exact calculations, unanticipated problems might occur during restoration projects. For example, while replacing a roof, you may discover concealed damage to the underlying structure, necessitating additional repairs. To avoid such surprises, set aside a contingency budget of 10-20% of your entire renovation costs. This buffer allows you to handle unexpected expenses without jeopardizing your overall financial strategy.

Calculating The ROI Of Renovations

Once you have a thorough understanding of the costs

involved, you must assess the potential return on investment for your proposed renovations. Consider how each improvement will impact the property's rental income and total value. For example, replacing kitchen appliances may justify a higher rental fee, whereas substantial structural repairs may not provide the same return.

To determine the possible ROI, calculate the estimated increase in rental income and compare it to the overall remodeling expenditures. This study might help you decide which projects to pursue based on their financial impact.

Calculating renovation and repair costs is an important part of successful rental property investment. By precisely estimating expenses, prioritizing essential renovations, and assessing possible returns, you may position yourself for long-term success in the competitive rental market.

MAKING AN OFFER AND CLOSING THE DEAL

Creating A Competitive Offer

Navigating the complexities of making a competitive bid in the real estate market is an important step toward obtaining your investment property. A well-crafted offer not only demonstrates your seriousness as a buyer, but it also places you well among other potential purchasers. Understanding the aspects that make an offer competitive will allow you to make more educated judgments and increase your chances of closing the business effectively.

Understanding market conditions

Before making an offer, understand the current market conditions. Are you in a buyer's market, where supply surpasses demand, or a seller's market, with limited inventory and several purchasers competing for the same properties? In a seller's market, competition can be severe, and your offer must stand out to pique the seller's interest. In contrast, in a buyer's market, you may have more bargaining power to secure advantageous conditions.

For example, if you learn that properties in your preferred location are selling quickly and frequently for more than the asking price, you may need to make a strong initial offer. On the other side, if a home has been on the market for a long time, you may have the opportunity to negotiate a lower price or better conditions.

Researching Comparable Sales

Conducting extensive research on comparable sales, often known as "comps," is an essential component of developing a competitive offer. Comps are properties that have recently sold in the same area and are comparable in size, condition, and characteristics to the one you are interested in. Analyzing these sales might provide useful insight into the property's fair market worth and help you decide a reasonable offer price.

For example, if you discover that similar properties in the neighborhood are selling for $300,000 to $320,000, you may decide to offer somewhat below this range if the property needs repairs or has been on the market for some time. In contrast, if your preferred property has distinctive qualities that are in high demand, a bigger offer may be required to close the purchase.

Include Strategic Contingencies

When making an offer, make sure to include strategic contingencies that protect your interests while also appealing to the seller. Common contingencies include finance, inspections, and appraisals. While they are necessary precautions, excessive contingencies can undermine your offer, particularly in a competitive market.

For example, having an inspection contingency is common practice, allowing you to withdraw if substantial problems are discovered during the inspection. However, in a competitive bidding situation, you may consider waiving this contingency or offering a limited timeframe for completion to demonstrate your commitment while safeguarding your interests.

Creating an Attractive Offer Price.

An enticing offer price strikes a balance between your budget and the property's market worth. It is critical to propose an offer that accurately reflects the property's value while also taking into account your financial objectives. Setting a competitive but not unreasonably high offer price allows for bargaining.

Consider how much you're willing to pay while accounting for prospective repair costs, estimated cash flow, and overall return on investment. If you are willing to pay somewhat more than the asking price due to great demand, make sure that your financial analysis supports your decision.

Presenting Your Offer

Once you've decided on your offer price and contingencies, it's time to deliver it. Collaborate with your real estate agent to create a professional offer letter that reflects your interest and dedication. The way you present your offer might have a big impact on how the seller perceives it.

Including a personal touch, such as a note to the seller explaining why you love their house and your vision for it, might help your offer stand out. Sellers typically like knowing that their home will be maintained for by someone who values it, which may influence their choice in your favor.

Negotiating terms and conditions

Prepare to negotiate after you've presented your offer. The seller may respond with a counter-offer or attempt to negotiate specific parameters. Understanding the important negotiating terms and conditions, such as closing fees, move-in dates, and included furnishings, will help you stay flexible during the negotiation process.

Maintain open contact with your real estate agent during negotiations, as they may assist you in navigating talks and advocating for your best interests. Be willing to compromise while remaining focused on your investment goals. For example, if the seller is adamant on the price but agrees to fund closing fees, this arrangement may still meet your financial goals.

Understanding the Closing Process

When your offer is approved, the closing process starts. This stage consists of various procedures, including obtaining money, conducting inspections, and finalizing legal papers. Understanding the closing timetable and duties can help to ensure that the transaction goes smoothly.

Throughout this period, stay organized and keep track of crucial dates and criteria. Collaborate with your lender, real estate agent, and attorney to ensure that all components of the closing process are completed efficiently. Preparing ahead of time will help you navigate any obstacles and avoid delays.

Creating a competitive offer necessitates a strategic strategy that includes research, market understanding, and good communication. Understanding market dynamics, completing thorough research on comparable transactions, considering strategic contingencies, and delivering an attractive offer will help you represent yourself as a serious buyer in the real estate market. Engaging in careful discussions and preparation for the closing process can help you obtain your investment property effectively.

Negotiating the Purchase Price.

Negotiating the purchase price is a critical phase in the real estate investment process. It's the art of striking a balance between what you're willing to pay and what the seller is willing to accept, and it takes a combination of strategy, market knowledge, and good communication. This chapter delves into the complexities of negotiation, preparing you to approach discussions with confidence and reach a successful solution.

Understanding the Seller's Perspective

To negotiate effectively, it is critical to understand the seller's motivation. Are they trying to sell quickly due to a job transfer or financial reasons, or are they just testing the market? Recognizing the seller's condition can provide useful information about how flexible they may be on price.

For example, if the seller is under time constraints and has already acquired another house, they may be more willing to accept a lower offer. A seller who does not have an urgent need to sell, on the other hand, may negotiate a higher price. Engaging in a chat with the seller or their agent can reveal these intentions, providing you an advantage during negotiations.

Researching Comparable Sales

Before commencing talks, conduct extensive research on comparable sales in the region. Analyzing recently sold properties with similar attributes to the one you're interested in gives a baseline for determining a fair price. This data provides you with real facts to back up your offer.

For example, if similar homes in the neighborhood sold for $280,000 but the seller wants $300,000, you have a strong case for bargaining down to a more affordable price. Presenting this information to the seller might strengthen your case by demonstrating your market knowledge and emphasizing that your offer is based on real data rather than random numbers.

Making an Initial Offer

Crafting your first offer is both a science and an art. It should be competitive while also reflecting the research you have undertaken. In a hot market, coming in too low may result in losing the house to another buyer. In contrast, an extremely high offer may leave little room for bargaining.

When delivering your initial offer, it is helpful to explain the logic behind your price. This could involve referring to similar sales data, any anticipated repairs, or market trends that support your valuation. By doing so, you not only defend your offer but also engage the seller in a discussion regarding the property's worth.

Navigating Counteroffers

In most circumstances, the seller will respond with a counteroffer, which is where talks can become more complicated. Be prepared for back-and-forth negotiations with many rounds of counteroffers. Patience and flexibility are essential during this stage.

When you receive a counteroffer, compare it to your initial offer and budget. Consider what factors are most essential to you—are you willing to haggle the price, or are other parameters, such as closing expenses or timetables, more important? For example, if the seller is set on the price but prepared to cover closing fees, the transaction may still meet your financial goals, making it a good deal.

Use Contingencies to Strengthen Your Position

Contingencies can help you negotiate more effectively while also protecting your interests. Inspection, appraisal, and finance contingencies are among the most common types. While they are common in real estate transactions, being strategic about them might help you get better deals.

For example, if you believe the seller is motivated but concerned about your offer price, you might recommend removing the inspection contingency in exchange for a larger offer that demonstrates your confidence in the property. However, you must carefully consider this decision, as it may expose you to unanticipated consequences in the future.

Developing Win-Win Scenarios

Negotiation is more than just getting the greatest price; it also entails creating solutions that benefit both sides. Striving for a win-win situation can help to smooth out the transaction and establish goodwill, which is especially crucial if issues arise later in the process.

For example, if the seller is hesitant to negotiate the price but wants to close soon, you could offer to postpone the closing date in exchange for a little reduction in the purchase price. This strategy indicates your willingness to compromise while still promoting your financial objectives.

Effective Communication and Relationship Building

Throughout the negotiation process, excellent communication is critical. Maintaining a respectful and professional manner leads to a positive relationship with the seller or their agent. Clear and honest communication can help avoid misconceptions and lead to more effective negotiations.

For example, if a specific concern develops about the property, such as necessary repairs, address it swiftly and gently. Instead of making demands, express your issues as inquiry. This method encourages collaboration rather than confrontation, resulting in a climate conducive to achieving an agreement.

Closing the gap

As discussions go, try to reduce the difference between your offer and the seller's asking price. This may need imaginative solutions, such as changing the conditions of the offer or paying earnest money to demonstrate your commitment. The idea is to design a path to agreement while staying within your budget.

Ultimately, successful negotiating requires a combination of preparation, market knowledge, and interpersonal skills. Understanding the seller's point of view, completing thorough research, developing a convincing offer, and keeping open communication can help you navigate the negotiating process efficiently and secure the property at a price that meets your investment objectives.

Navigating The Closing Process

The closing procedure is the final step in becoming a rental property owner. It is a comprehensive procedure that necessitates meticulous attention to detail, prompt decision-making, and clear communication among all parties involved. Successfully navigating this essential phase will guarantee that you complete the transaction smoothly and can confidently assume your new role as a property investor.

Understanding the Closing Timeline

The time it takes to close on a property depends on a number of factors, including the conditions negotiated in your purchase agreement, the type of financing used, and the specific needs of your local market. Typically, the closing procedure takes between 30 and 60 days. Understanding the timeline is critical because it allows you to properly prepare for each step along the road.

As the closing date approaches, you'll need to coordinate a number of chores, including confirming your financing, conducting any necessary inspections, and ensuring that all documentation is in place. A well-organized timeline will help you stay on track and avoid last-minute surprises.

Reviewing Closing Costs

Closing fees can have a big impact on your overall investment budget, therefore it is critical to understand what these costs are. These fees may include title insurance, appraisal fees, attorney fees, recording fees, and transfer taxes, among others. Typically, closing charges range between 2% and 5% of the purchase price.

During the negotiation phase, you might debate who will bear these costs—the buyer, the seller, or a combination of the two. For example, if you agree on a higher purchase price, you could ask the seller to contribute to your closing fees. Being aware of these charges will allow you to make strategic decisions and improve your negotiating position.

Conducting a last walk-through

Before sealing the sale, many buyers fail to undertake a final walk-through of the property. This walk-through allows you to confirm that the property is in the condition specified in the contract and that any repairs promised by the seller have been done.

During your inspection, pay particular attention to any changes in the property's condition from your first visit. For example, if the seller promised to fix a leaking faucet or replace damaged flooring, ensure that the repairs were completed satisfactorily. If you identify any difficulties, you have the opportunity to fix them before the closing, perhaps delaying the process until they are rectified.

Understanding The Closing Documents

As the closing date approaches, you will be presented with a number of documents that need to be carefully reviewed and signed. Familiarizing yourself with these documents will not only help you comprehend the transaction, but will also provide you the ability to ask educated questions.

The key documents you'll encounter include:

1. Closing Disclosure: This document summarizes the final details of your mortgage, such as the loan amount, interest rate, monthly payments, and any closing charges. Please review this paper carefully to ensure that it meets your expectations.

2. Deed of Trust: This instrument secures the loan by creating a lien on the property, giving the lender the right to take ownership if you fail to repay the debt.

3. Bill of Sale: If personal property, such as appliances or furniture, is included in the sale, this document will list it.

4. Title Transfer Documents: These ensure that ownership of the property passes from the seller to you, establishing your legal claim to it.

Taking the time to read and understand these materials will help to avoid future confusion and concerns. Don't be afraid to ask your real estate agent or attorney to clarify anything that appears ambiguous.

Working with professionals

Throughout the closing process, you will work with a variety of experts, such as real estate agents, attorneys, bankers, and title companies. Each side plays an important role in ensuring a successful transaction, and open communication is essential.

Your real estate agent will walk you through the closing process, answering questions and providing insight into what you might expect. An attorney can help analyze legal documents and ensure compliance with local laws, while your lender will handle the financing.

Establishing positive relationships with these specialists can result in a smoother closing process. For example, if your attorney is proactive and interacts well with the title firm, any inconsistencies can be resolved promptly.

Finalizing the Transaction

Prepare to spend many hours at the closing table, signing various paperwork and finalizing the transaction. Bring your proper identity, any necessary funds (typically a cashier's check), and a good attitude.

Take the time to read over each document before signing

it and ask for clarification on any points you don't understand. This is your opportunity to confirm that everything is in line with the agreement.

Once all of the documentation are signed, the title firm will record the deed and the seller will receive the profits of the transaction. You will then be given the keys to your new home, signalling the official transfer of ownership.

Post-closing considerations

After closing, there are a few important tasks to do as you begin your new position as a landlord. First, create a property management plan that includes how you will handle tenant applications, screening, and leasing processes. You should also make sure that any immediate repairs or upgrades are completed before the tenants come in.

Also, update your homeowners insurance coverage to reflect your new property ownership. This is critical for protecting your money from unforeseen circumstances. You may also want to set aside funds for ongoing maintenance and improvements to keep your rental property in top condition.

Navigating the closing process may appear overwhelming, but with good planning, attention to detail, and a strong team of specialists on your side, you can successfully complete this final step and begin your adventure as a rental property investor. Accept the opportunity to accumulate money and attain financial independence through real estate, knowing that you have successfully completed one of the most important transactions of your life.

PREPARING YOUR PROPERTY FOR TENANTS
Renovations and Upgrades

Transforming your rental property into a pleasant home for tenants is critical to increasing rental income and ensuring long-term occupancy. This chapter digs into the renovations and enhancements that can dramatically improve your property's appeal while also offering a good return on investment. By deliberately focusing on the right upgrades, you may attract high-quality tenants while keeping the property's value.

Understanding Tenants' Expectations

Today's tenants have particular expectations for rental houses. Many people want modern conveniences, energy efficiency, and comfortable living areas that feel like home. Understanding these preferences might help you prioritize repairs that meet tenant requests. Conducting market research in your area can reveal which features are most popular, allowing you to make educated upgrade selections.

Important Renovations To Consider

Certain upgrades can significantly improve both the appearance and functionality of your property while preparing it for tenants. A new coat of paint is one of the simplest and most cost-effective methods to revitalize your space. Choose neutral hues that appeal to a wide range of people; this allows tenants to imagine their belongings in the space without feeling constrained by aggressive color schemes.

Updating fixtures is another significant makeover. Replacing old light fixtures, faucets, and cabinet handles may instantly update your home. These changes not only improve the appearance of the property, but they also show tenants that you are concerned about its upkeep.

Kitchen And Bathroom Upgrades

The kitchen and bathroom are two key factors that can affect a tenant's selection. Investing in kitchen remodeling might provide a significant return. Consider replacing old appliances with more energy-efficient models. These gadgets not only appeal to environmentally aware tenants, but they also reduce utility expenses, which is an appealing selling feature.

Simple improvements to the bathroom, such as replacing the vanity, laying new flooring, or adding modern fixtures, can significantly improve the space. Making sure these spaces are clean, practical, and visually appealing will help your house stand out in a competitive market.

Improving Energy Efficiency

With rising energy prices, tenants are increasingly looking for buildings that promote energy efficiency. Simple modifications, such as increasing insulation, sealing windows and doors, and adding programmable thermostats, can drastically reduce energy consumption. These upgrades not only save tenants' utility expenses, but they also promote sustainability, which many renters value today.

Consider installing energy-efficient lighting around the property. LED lights are a less expensive and more energy-efficient alternative to incandescent bulbs. Highlighting these energy-efficient features in your listings can attract environmentally aware tenants and differentiate your property from others on the market.

Increasing Curb Appeal

The façade of your property makes the initial impression on a potential tenant. Improving curb appeal can make a significant impact in attracting new tenants. Simple landscape modifications, such as mowing the lawn, planting flowers, or adding decorative elements like mulch and edging, can help to create a welcoming environment.

If your property has an outdoor area, consider making it both functional and appealing. Adding a patio, deck, or outdoor seating area can boost the property's value and popularity. Tenants are frequently drawn to areas where they may rest and entertain, so outdoor improvements are a smart investment.

Safety And Security Enhancements

Tenants prioritize safety, and investing in security

measures can help them feel certain that they are making the right decision. Consider adding security elements like deadbolt locks, motion-sensor lighting, and surveillance cameras. These upgrades not only provide peace of mind, but also show your dedication to tenant safety.

Updating smoke and carbon monoxide detectors is also critical. Ensure that these devices are functional and in accordance with local regulations. Highlighting these safety elements while promoting your property might help to foster confidence and attract responsible tenants.

Budgeting For Renovations

Before beginning any renovation job, it's critical to develop a reasonable budget. Examine your finances and evaluate how much you can spend on upgrades without risking your investment. Prioritize upgrades that have the most impact for the lowest cost, and consider getting bids from various contractors to guarantee you get the best deal.

While some renovations can be completed on their own, larger projects may require the assistance of professionals to ensure quality craftsmanship. Keep in mind that making costs can result in problems down the road, perhaps costing you more in repairs and tenant turnover.

Timing Your Renovations

The timing of your renovations can significantly influence your rental strategy. If possible, schedule improvements during low-demand periods, such as the winter months, when fewer tenants are actively looking for a property. This strategy allows you to perform critical upgrades without affecting present renters, reducing vacancy time.

Additionally, organizing renovations prior to advertising the house for rent might provide a significant marketing advantage. Having a clean, move-in-ready home can attract tenants fast, resulting in less downtime between rentals and higher income flow.

Setting the Proper Rent Price

Determining the appropriate rental pricing for your property is critical to attracting and retaining great renters while maintaining a successful investment. Setting the appropriate rent necessitates a careful balancing of market conditions, property characteristics, and financial objectives. This chapter discusses what elements to consider when pricing your rental property, how to examine the rental market, and how to make informed decisions that benefit both you and your prospective tenants.

Understanding Market Dynamics

To create a competitive rent pricing, you must first

understand the dynamics of your local rental market. This technique relies heavily on market research. Begin by examining comparable properties, sometimes known as "comps," which are similar rental units in your area. Look for properties that are comparable to yours in terms of size, amenities, condition, and location. This comparison research allows you to determine the going rate for comparable rentals, giving you a strong foundation for setting your own price.

For example, if you own a two-bedroom apartment with contemporary finishes and facilities, look into other two-bedroom condos within a mile radius. Take note of their rental costs, features, and any unique selling factors they may have. This information can help you choose a competitive but fair rental pricing for your property.

Factors Influencing Rent Prices

Several factors determine the rental price you may charge. Consider the elements listed below:

1. location: Properties in desirable neighborhoods with strong schools, low crime rates, and easy access to amenities usually command higher rentals. If your home is located in an up-and-coming neighborhood or near public transportation, it may attract tenants ready to pay a higher price for convenience.

2. Property Conditions: A well-maintained property with modern upgrades will naturally command a higher rent than one that needs extensive repairs or updates.

Highlight any upgrades or enhancements you've made, such as new appliances or fresh paint, which helps explain a higher selling price.

3. Market Trends: Stay current on area rental trends. If there is a high demand for rentals and a low availability, you may be able to boost your rate. Conversely, during instances of economic depression or oversupply, you may need to lower your expectations in order to remain competitive.

4. Amenities and Features: Properties with desirable amenities—such as in-unit laundry, off-street parking, a swimming pool, or outdoor spaces—usually attract higher rentals. When selling your property, make sure to highlight these amenities because they significantly improve the renting experience.

Calculating Your Rent Price

Once you have a solid understanding of market dynamics and the elements that influence rent rates, you can start estimating the right rent for your home. A common way is to calculate the price per square foot. To establish a baseline value, divide the rent prices of comparable properties by their square footage.

For example, if a nearby apartment of comparable quality rents for $2,000 and contains 1,000 square feet, the cost per square foot is $2.00. If your property is 1,200 square feet, multiplying the price per square foot by your square footage yields a proposed rent of approximately $2,400. However, this is only one way; it should be used in conjunction with your previous study and comprehension of the topics discussed.

Testing The Market

Once you've determined a prospective rental price, testing the market can provide useful information. List your home for the proposed rent and assess the response. If you receive a lot of interest and queries, it could mean that your pricing is appropriate. However, if you discover that your property is not attracting applicants or generating little interest, it may be time to reconsider your pricing plan.

Consider arranging open houses or viewings to gather tenant feedback. Take note of any criticism from prospective tenants regarding the rent pricing or comparable listings with cheaper prices. Flexibility in your pricing plan might result in faster occupancy, lower vacancy expenses, and lost revenue.

Incorporating Incentives

In highly competitive rental markets, providing incentives might help you stand out. If you find yourself in a scenario where you need to cut the rent to attract tenants, consider offering incentives that provide value without adversely affecting your bottom line. For example, you may provide one month of free rent or include utilities in the rental amount. These strategies can entice tenants and create a sense of urgency, causing them to prefer your property over others.

Legal And Ethical Considerations

It is critical to follow local laws and regulations regarding rental pricing. Familiarize yourself with any rent control rules in your area, which may limit how much you can charge or how frequently you can raise the rent. Transparency and fairness in your pricing procedures not only foster trust among potential tenants, but also help you maintain a positive reputation as a landlord.

When determining the rent price, keep your desired tenant demographic in mind. Understanding their financial capabilities and expectations will allow you to strike the correct balance. Overcharging may result in extended vacancies, whereas undercharging may reduce the overall value of your investment.

Setting the appropriate rent price requires a combination of research, strategy, and an understanding of market dynamics.

Marketing Your Rental Property

Successfully marketing your rental property is critical for getting excellent tenants immediately. In a competitive rental market, good marketing methods might be the difference between filling your vacancy and increasing your rental income. This chapter delves into several tactics and tools for promoting your property, targeting the relevant demographic, and generating interest from potential tenants.

Creating an Engaging Listing

A fascinating listing is the starting point for any effective rental property marketing strategy. Your listing needs to be informative, engaging, and visually appealing. Begin by drafting a fascinating description that highlights your property's distinguishing qualities and benefits. Use descriptive language to create a clear picture of the living area, stressing essential features like openness, natural light, and modern finishes.

For example, rather than typing, "Two-bedroom apartment," try this: "Experience the charm of this sun-drenched two-bedroom apartment featuring high ceilings, hardwood floors, and a spacious open-concept layout, perfect for entertaining friends or enjoying quiet evenings at home."

Also, make sure your listing includes important facts like the number of bedrooms and bathrooms, square footage, rental fee, leasing terms, and any included utilities. Set clear expectations for possible tenants by being open and honest about any rules or restrictions, such as pet policy or smoking bans.

Using high-quality photography

A picture is worth a thousand words, especially on the rental market. High-quality photos can dramatically improve your listing and attract attention to your home. Consider hiring a professional real estate photographer to showcase your property in the best possible light.

Highlight the most appealing aspects of your property, such as the kitchen, living room, and outdoor spaces. Make sure each space is well-lit, decluttered, and set to create a welcoming feel. Including photographs of the neighborhood or surrounding attractions might also help prospective tenants visualize their lifestyle in the region.

Leveraging Online Platforms

In today's digital age, online channels are quite useful for marketing rental properties. Listing your property on prominent rental platforms like Zillow, Apartments.com, and Craigslist will greatly increase your reach. Each platform has its unique audience, therefore it's best to use many sites to increase visibility.

Consider setting up a specialized website or social media page for your rental property. This platform allows you to display extra photographs, detailed information, and tenant testimonials, giving potential customers a complete picture of what you provide. Social media outlets such as Facebook, Instagram, and Twitter enable customized advertising, allowing you to promote your property to certain demographics in your area.

Networking and word-of-mouth

When it comes to marketing your rental property, don't

overlook the value of personal connections. Inform relatives, family, and colleagues that you have a property available for rent. Word of mouth might result in recommendations from those who know potential tenants looking for accommodation.

Joining local community groups or internet forums can also help you connect with persons looking for rental properties. Engaging with your community will help you not only find possible tenants, but also improve your reputation as a landlord.

Hosting Open Houses

Open houses are a great opportunity to display your property and attract potential tenants. Schedule a time for interested tenants to view the property, ask questions, and get a sense of the space. To maximize attendance, promote your open house using internet listings, social media, and community bulletin boards.

Create a welcoming atmosphere at the open house. Consider offering beverages and informational booklets that describe the property's characteristics, neighboring facilities, and your contact information. Engaging with visitors, addressing their inquiries, and emphasizing your property's distinguishing attributes can make a lasting impression.

Highlighting the Local Amenities

Potential tenants frequently seek residences that provide

convenience and access to local amenities. When marketing your rental, make sure to include nearby attractions like parks, schools, retail malls, and public transportation alternatives.

For example, if your home is near a prominent park or recreational area, emphasize how it improves the living experience. Perhaps you'd say, "Just steps away from the vibrant Central Park, this apartment offers not only a beautiful living space but also quick access to nature trails, picnic areas, and weekend farmers' markets."

Responding Quickly to Inquiries

Once your marketing efforts have generated interest, it is critical to reply quickly to questions from potential tenants. Timely communication indicates professionalism and establishes a favorable tone in your landlord-tenant relationship. Be prepared to answer questions regarding the property, the application process, and the lease agreement.

To streamline your communication, consider utilizing a uniform answer template for common inquiries. This efficiency can make a big difference in attracting tenants, especially since many prospective renters may be looking at many properties at the same time.

Using Tenant Screening Services

As you attract potential tenants, it is critical to execute a rigorous tenant screening procedure. This process ensures that you choose trustworthy tenants who will respect your property and keep their lease requirements. Consider using tenant screening services, which include background checks, credit reports, and rental history evaluations.

When marketing your property, highlight your commitment to thorough screening as a selling factor, ensuring prospective renters that they will be living in a community of responsible people.

Marketing your rental property efficiently necessitates a deliberate approach that combines captivating descriptions, high-quality visuals, and the appropriate venues for reaching potential tenants. By highlighting your property's unique characteristics, utilizing community connections, and keeping open communication, you may successfully recruit quality tenants who will appreciate and care for your investment.

MANAGING YOUR RENTAL PROPERTIES

Finding and Screening Tenants

The tenants you choose to live in your rental home will have a significant impact on its performance. Finding the proper tenants might be the difference between a pleasant, successful renting experience and one filled with complications. This chapter delves into successful techniques for acquiring great tenants, as well as critical elements in the tenant screening process to help you make informed selections.

Creating a Tenant Friendly Listing

Your search for the ideal tenant begins with an enticing listing that appropriately describes your home. A well-written advertisement not only defines the property, but also expresses the type of renter you are seeking. Highlight aspects that will appeal to prospective tenants, such as modern appliances, roomy layouts, and surrounding facilities. For example, if your rental is in a bustling neighborhood with excellent schools and parks, include this in your ad to attract families and young professionals.

Consider utilizing fascinating words to elicit an emotional response. Instead of just saying "two-bedroom apartment," you may say "Discover your sanctuary in this beautifully renovated two-bedroom apartment, where modern comforts meet charming neighborhood vibes." Including high-quality images will further improve your listing, highlighting the property's best features.

Using Multiple Platforms

In today's digital age, casting a wide net is critical for attracting potential tenants. Post your rental listing on prominent rental websites like Zillow, Apartments.com, and Craigslist, where many potential tenants start their search. Additionally, social media sites can be extremely useful for spreading the news. Sharing your listing on Facebook or Instagram, as well as urging your network to share it, can dramatically enhance the visibility of your home.

Consider contacting local community groups or forums dedicated to housing or rents. Engaging with these online forums can help you connect with people who are actively looking for rental options. Furthermore, don't underestimate the effectiveness of classic approaches like "For Rent" signs in front of the property or leaflets at local businesses.

Installing a Screening Process

When you start receiving questions about your rental property, it's important to start a thorough tenant screening process. Screening is essential for locating dependable tenants who will pay their rent on time and care for your home. The first step in the screening process is to establish specific criteria for prospective tenants. This may include minimum income restrictions, renting history, and credit score thresholds.

Clearly explain your screening criteria in your listing to attract the correct individuals from the start. This clarity saves you time while also setting expectations for applicants.

Application Forms and Background Checks

After receiving applications, give potential tenants a common application form to ensure you collect consistent information. The application should include important information including employment history, renting history, and references.

Once you have received completed applications, it is time to conduct background checks. Credit checks, criminal background checks, and employment and rental history verification are all common parts of this process. Many property management organizations provide screening services that simplify the procedure and provide detailed data.

For example, a possible tenant with a good credit history and favorable rental references is likely to be a lower-risk candidate than someone with a history of late payments or evictions. You may make informed decisions about who to welcome onto your property by carefully reviewing this information.

Conducting interviews and reference checks

After you've narrowed down your pool of applicants, conducting interviews can provide significant information about their appropriateness as tenants. Use this opportunity to ask open-ended questions about their rental history, motivations for moving, and expectations for the home.

Furthermore, contacting references from former landlords or employers can offer information on the applicant's dependability and personality. For example, if a past landlord compliments an applicant on their timely rent payments and respectful manner, it is a good sign of their potential as a renter.

In contrast, if references disclose difficulties such as frequent late payments or complaints about property damage, it may be prudent to evaluate the applicant.

Make the Final Decision

Once you've done interviews and obtained all of the essential information, you may make your decision. Trust your intuition and the evidence you've gathered. A responsible tenant not only satisfies your requirements, but also matches your expectations as a landlord.

When you've found a tenant, announce the good news right away and start preparing for the lease. Make sure you provide clear directions for the next stages, such as obtaining a security deposit and setting up a move-in date. This proactive communication establishes a healthy landlord-tenant connection from the start.

Finding and screening renters is an important part of operating your rental property. Create an appealing listing, use several platforms, conduct a thorough screening procedure, and communicate effectively to attract responsible tenants who will contribute to a successful and profitable rental experience. Taking the time to locate the best fit for your home will result in a smoother and more satisfying investment journey.

Handling Lease Agreements and Security Deposits

Navigating the complexities of lease agreements and security deposits is an important part of successfully managing your rental property. These elements not only protect your investment, but also set the stage for a pleasant landlord-tenant relationship. Understanding how to establish clear lease agreements and efficiently manage security deposits can assist ensure a smooth leasing process and protect your interests.

The Significance Of A Well-Crafted Lease Agreement

A lease agreement is more than a formal document; it is a legally binding contract that specifies the terms and circumstances of the renting arrangement. A well-written lease serves several important goals, including protecting your rights as a landlord, setting clear expectations for your tenants, and providing a framework for addressing potential conflicts.

When writing a lease agreement, it is critical to include all relevant data to avoid misunderstandings. Begin by explicitly identifying the rental property's address, lease period (month-to-month or fixed-term lease), and rent amount. Specify when the rent is due and the allowed methods of payment, such as cheque, bank transfer, or an online payment platform. This clarity allows tenants to better understand their obligations and avoids confusion regarding payment dates.

Key Elements of a Lease Agreement

In addition to basic rental information, your lease agreement should include many crucial provisions. Consider include sections addressing the following:

1. Occupancy Limit: Specify the maximum number of occupants permitted in the rental unit. This reduces overcrowding and guarantees compliance with local housing restrictions.

2) Pet Policy: Clearly specify whether pets are permitted and any accompanying limitations, such as breed restrictions or additional pet deposits. For example, if your property is pet-friendly but has certain conditions, include these in the lease to avoid future issues.

3. Maintenance Responsibilities: Clarify the landlord and tenant's duties for property maintenance. For example, you may state that tenants are responsible for minor

repairs and upkeep while you handle major repairs and maintenance issues.

4. Termination Conditions: Include details on lease termination, renewal alternatives, and the notice period required by both parties. This section establishes expectations regarding what happens at the conclusion of the lease, so avoiding surprises.

5. Legal Compliance: Make sure your lease complies with local, state, and federal regulations. For example, if you live in an area with unique tenant protection laws, your lease must include such restrictions to avoid legal difficulties.

Collecting Security Deposits

A security deposit provides a financial safety for landlords by covering any damages or unpaid rent when a renter vacates the property. Collecting a security deposit upfront is common practice, but it is critical to execute the procedure honestly and properly.

When determining the size of the security deposit, take into account local rules that govern the maximum permissible deposit. Many countries cap security deposits at one or two months' rent, so make sure your deposit amount meets these requirements. Once you've determined the deposit amount, make sure you clearly express it to prospective tenants in the lease agreement.

Documenting The Condition Of The Property

Before the tenants move in, make a complete walkthrough of the property and document its condition. Take careful photos of each room, noting any wear and tear. Keeping a comprehensive record of the property's condition at the start of the lease will help to avoid arguments when the tenant moves out.

Give the tenant a copy of the move-in inspection report and request their signature to certify their understanding of the property's condition. This stage promotes openness while emphasizing the significance of returning the property in excellent condition.

Managing Security Deposits Throughout the Lease

Maintain open contact with your tenants about the security deposit throughout the life of the lease. If any repairs or maintenance are required during their tenancy, address how these concerns will affect their deposit when they move out. For example, if a renter complains about a leaking faucet and you arrange for repairs, tell them that ordinary maintenance will not damage their security deposit.

Additionally, remind tenants of their responsibilities to maintain the property in good condition. Providing periodic reminders about proper upkeep and swiftly responding to maintenance requests will assist maintain the property and minimize deposit disputes when it comes time to move out.

Return of Security Deposit After Tenancy

When the tenant's lease expires, it is critical to undertake a comprehensive inspection of the property to identify any damage that exceeds regular wear and tear. Use your initial documentation to compare the property's state at the time of move-in to its condition when you move out. If there are any damages that need to be repaired, assess the cost and deduct it from the security deposit.

Remember to follow local rules about the period for recovering security deposits. Many countries require landlords to repay the deposit within a certain time frame—typically 30 days—along with an itemized description of any deductions. Even with deductions, providing openness and clear paperwork helps to develop trust with your tenants.

Clear Communication Is Important

Communication is essential when dealing with lease agreements and security deposits. Maintain open channels of contact with your tenants, and respond swiftly to any queries or complaints. A positive connection based on trust and transparency can assist to avoid issues and make the renting experience more enjoyable for both sides.

Mastering the art of lease agreements and security deposit management allows you to protect your investment while maintaining a respectful and professional relationship with your tenants. Taking the effort to establish precise terms and conditions will not only safeguard your rights, but will also pave the way for a positive renting experience.

Managing Repairs and Maintenance

Effective management of repairs and maintenance is essential for effective rental property management. It not only protects the value of your investment, but also improves tenant satisfaction and retention. A proactive approach to maintenance concerns can help you establish strong relationships with your tenants while also keeping your home a desirable place to live.

Importance of Regular Maintenance

Regular maintenance is critical for avoiding larger, more expensive repairs down the road. By implementing a proactive maintenance routine, you can detect possible problems before they worsen. For example, performing seasonal checks on your home can help you detect problems such as roof leaks, plumbing issues, or HVAC failures early on. This technique not only saves you money in the long term, but it also helps you keep your tenants happy, who value living in a well-kept environment.

Setting a Maintenance Schedule

Creating a maintenance schedule might help to manage repairs and upkeep more efficiently. This program should include typical tasks like changing air filters, repairing appliances, and testing smoke detectors. For example, you could plan an HVAC inspection twice a year, prior to the cooling and heating seasons. Prioritizing these chores can help you avoid system failures and keep your tenants pleasant.

Seasonal maintenance duties, such as gutter cleaning in the fall and grass care in the spring, should also be on your plan. Planning these actions ahead of time allows you to better allocate resources and avoid last-minute emergencies.

Responding To Tenant Requests

Tenants are your eyes and ears when it comes to detecting maintenance problems. Encouraging them to report problems quickly is critical for good property management. Make it easy for tenants to express their issues, whether via an online portal, email, or phone call. When a renter reports a maintenance issue, respond promptly and recognize their request. For example, if a renter reports a leaking faucet, notify them that you have received their request and will have an expert inspect it shortly.

Timely communication fosters trust and makes tenants feel appreciated. It is critical to implement a system for tracking maintenance requests and their response status. Consider employing property management software that can help you manage and track these requests effectively. This way, you can ensure that no issues are neglected and repairs are handled on time.

Choosing the Right Contractors.

When it comes to repairs, the contractor you choose can have a big impact on the quality of the work and tenant satisfaction. Creating a network of dependable contractors is critical for successful property management. Seek referrals from other landlords or real estate experts, and extensively research potential contractors' licensing, insurance, and reviews. For example, if a tenant reports a plumbing problem, having a reliable plumber on speed dial can speed up the resolution process and reduce discomfort for your tenants.

When picking contractors, take into account not only their qualifications but also their communication style and attentiveness. A contractor that communicates effectively and arrives on time will reflect positively on you as a landlord.

Managing Emergency Repairs

Emergency repairs necessitate quick action and clear communication. Define what constitutes an emergency for your tenants, such as concerns with plumbing, heating, or electrical systems. When an emergency occurs, having a strategy in place might allow you to respond more efficiently. For example, if a pipe bursts in the middle of the night, make sure tenants understand how to contact you or a designated emergency contact.

In addition, have a list of reliable emergency contractors who can respond immediately to urgent situations. This proactive strategy not only helps to mitigate harm, but it also demonstrates your dedication to tenant welfare.

Keeping Open Communication With Tenants

Establishing open contact with your tenants is essential for managing repairs and maintenance. Encourage tenants to submit feedback on the property's condition and any concerns they have. Regular check-ins might help you detect potential maintenance concerns before they become major problems.

For example, after finishing a repair, check in with the tenant to ensure they are satisfied with the job done. This demonstrates that you value their feedback and are dedicated to upholding a high level for your property.

Documentation and Record Keeping

Keeping detailed records of all maintenance requests, repairs, and expenses is critical to good property management. Document each tenant request, including the date it was received, the nature of the problem, and how it was handled. This record-keeping not only keeps you organized, but it also provides useful information for taxes and future decisions.

Additionally, keeping receipts and invoices for repairs and upkeep can assist you in tracking your spending and determining the overall profitability of your rental property. If a specific problem occurs repeatedly, it may suggest the need for a more significant upgrade or replacement, which will guide your long-term maintenance approach.

Budget for Repairs and Maintenance

Setting up a percentage of your rental income for repairs and maintenance is critical to financial security. Experts frequently propose setting aside 1% of the property's value each year for upkeep charges. This fund will enable you to handle unforeseen repairs without depleting your total financial flow.

Consider setting up a separate maintenance reserve fund, which may be especially useful for larger needs like repairing a roof or upgrading an HVAC system. You can avoid financial stress and maintain your property in good shape by budgeting for these expenses ahead of time.

Managing repairs and maintenance correctly is critical for increasing the value of your rental property while maintaining tenant happiness. By taking a proactive approach, communicating clearly with tenants, and keeping precise records, you may confidently negotiate the challenges of property upkeep

BUILDING WEALTH AND EXPANDING YOUR PORTFOLIO

Reinvesting Your Profits

As you begin your adventure into rental property investing, the prospect of reinvesting your gains can be both thrilling and intimidating. It's a technique that not only increases your wealth-building potential, but also sets you up for long-term success in the real estate market. The objective is to understand how to successfully reinvest your earnings to build a long-term, lucrative portfolio.

The Power Of Compounding

Reinvesting profits takes advantage of compounding, which generates additional money over time. Just as interest compounds in a savings account, reinvesting gains in real estate ventures makes your money work harder for you. For example, if you receive $10,000 in rental income one year and reinvest it in another property, your future rental income may double or even quadruple, depending on how well the property performs.

Consider the following scenario: a real estate investor successfully manages a single-family rental and wishes to reinvest the income in acquiring a multifamily property. The rental income from a multifamily apartment can far exceed that of a single-family home, demonstrating how reinvesting can result in exponential growth in cash flow.

Strategic Property Acquisition

One of the most successful strategies to reinvest your money is to purchase additional homes. However, it is critical to do this intelligently. Investigate potential locations and property types that correspond with your investing objectives. For example, if your first property is a single-family home in a growing neighborhood, consider increasing your portfolio by purchasing a duplex or triplex in the same region.

Additionally, diversifying your portfolio helps reduce risk. If your early investments are primarily in residential properties, consider looking into commercial real estate or vacation rentals. Each property type has its own market dynamics and income potential, allowing for a more balanced approach to wealth creation.

Improving Existing Properties

Reinvesting doesn't just mean buying new properties; it also means enhancing your old ones. Kitchen renovations, bathroom upgrades, and garden improvements can all help to raise property value and rental income. A small investment in a kitchen remodel, for example, could result in a significant return if tenants are prepared to pay more for modern facilities.

Regularly assessing the state of your properties enables

you to find areas for improvement. This proactive approach keeps your properties competitive in the rental market, recruiting high-quality renters willing to pay higher rents.

Establishing A Reserve Fund

It is a good idea to set up a reserve fund when reinvesting gains. This financial cushion enables you to cover unexpected expenses, such as emergency repairs or vacancies, without affecting your investment plan. For example, if a major appliance malfunctions or a tenant unexpectedly vacates, having funds set aside might keep you from scrambling for cash or relying exclusively on rental revenue.

A frequent guideline is to save three to six months' worth of operating expenditures for each property in your reserve fund. This approach gives you piece of mind and helps you achieve your long-term growth goals.

Exploring Alternative Investments

Reinvesting your money also opens up new investment opportunities in the real estate market. Consider investing in real estate investment trusts (REITs) or crowdfunding sites. These choices enable you to diversify your investments beyond direct property ownership while still capitalizing on the real estate market's growth.

For example, if you have $50,000 in profits, putting a

portion of it in a REIT will give you exposure to a variety of real estate sectors, including commercial, industrial, and healthcare buildings. This diversification can improve your portfolio's stability and growth potential while reducing risk.

Networking And Education

As you look for reinvestment possibilities, your network can provide useful insights and resources. Attend real estate investment seminars, join local real estate associations, and meet experienced investors. Networking allows you to share ideas, learn about developing trends, and find investment opportunities that are not publicly disclosed.

Additionally, investing in your education is critical. Read books, take classes, and keep up with industry news to learn about market circumstances, financing choices, and best practices in property management. Knowledge is a strong instrument that can help you make better investments decisions and achieve higher profits.

Tax Strategy and Benefits

Understanding the tax implications of your investing strategy can have a big impact on your long-term financial performance. By reinvesting revenues in new properties or renovations, you may be eligible for tax breaks and perks, such as depreciation. This implies you can reduce your taxable income and maximize your profits.

For example, if you reinvest $20,000 in property upgrades, you can deduct the cost over several years, lowering your tax liability. Consulting with a real estate-experienced tax professional can help you understand these techniques and guarantee you're getting the most out of possible benefits.

Maintaining Discipline and Focus

While the potential for development is exciting, it is critical to maintain discipline and concentration in your reinvestment plan. Set specific financial goals and review your progress on a regular basis. Evaluate the performance of your properties, analyze market conditions, and change your reinvestment strategy as necessary.

For example, if a specific area exhibits indications of decline, you may want to shift your investing efforts to a more promising place. Staying aware of market changes and being willing to change your plan can lead to greater long-term success.

Creating A Legacy

Finally, reinvesting your gains in rental homes is more than just a financial benefit; it is also about leaving a legacy. As you build your portfolio and wealth, consider how your assets might benefit your family and community. By providing great housing, you are not only increasing your income; you are also improving the well-being of others and establishing a sense of stability.

Investing in rental properties can be a tremendous tool for wealth growth, but it needs careful preparation, a willingness to learn, and a dedication to reinvesting gains wisely. By focusing on strategic acquisitions, property upgrades, and diversifying your investments, you may build a strong portfolio that will expand over time, resulting in long-term financial security and riches.

Scaling Up: Acquiring Additional Properties

As you traverse the world of real estate investing, the concept of scaling up by purchasing more properties becomes an important part of your wealth-building plan. Expanding your portfolio can lead to new income sources, increased cash flow, and more equity. However, scaling up necessitates a deliberate approach, with each additional investment aligning with your financial objectives and improving your overall plan.

Understanding the Advantages of Scaling Up

The desire for financial expansion is often the driving force behind the choice to acquire new properties. Each new property is an opportunity to improve your income and equity. Assume you own a duplex that earns $2,000 in monthly rental income. If you buy another identical property, your monthly income might quadruple, leaving you with additional money to reinvest or save for future chances.

Additionally, owning many properties can help to reduce risk. If one of your properties becomes vacant or incurs unanticipated expenses, the revenue from your other properties can assist cover the costs. This diversification strengthens your financial basis, helping you to weather market volatility more efficiently.

Evaluating Your Financial Capability

Before commencing on the process of acquiring additional properties, it is critical to assess your financial situation. This includes evaluating your present income, expenses, and cash flow. Calculate your debt-to-income ratio to determine how much extra you can borrow. Lenders normally aim for a ratio of less than 36%, which means your overall loan commitments should not exceed 36% of your gross income.

For example, if your current rental properties generate a lot of cash flow, you may be able to get financing for new purchases easier. Maintaining a solid reserve money might also provide you peace of mind when taking on new properties. A well-prepared investor is more likely to capitalize on opportunities as they come.

Selecting the Right Properties

When scaling up, the choice of extra attributes is crucial. Begin by identifying markets with potential for growth. Examine economic data such as employment growth, population trends, and neighborhood amenities. For example, investing in a location with a thriving tech industry may result in a continual influx of tenants looking for rental homes.

It is also critical to analyze the types of properties that are compatible with your investing strategy. If your present portfolio consists mostly of single-family houses, you may want to look into multifamily or commercial real estate. Diversifying your property types can reduce risk while increasing your potential rewards.

For example, if you invest in a four-unit apartment complex in a busy neighborhood, you can generate various revenue streams. Each unit generates rental income, which boosts your overall cash flow while lowering the impact of vacancy.

Using Leverage Wisely.

One of the most powerful tools in real estate investing is leverage, which allows you to buy properties with borrowed money. By putting down a percentage of the property's value, you can get control of an asset worth significantly more than your initial investment. However, it is critical to wield leverage responsibly.

For example, if you buy a $300,000 home with a 20% down payment, your initial investment is $60,000. As the property appreciates over time, you benefit from the entire $300,000 asset value despite only investing $60,000. This technique can greatly increase your profits, but you must verify that your rental revenue covers your mortgage and other costs.

Performing Thorough Due Diligence

When considering acquiring additional properties, extensive due diligence is essential. This process entails inspecting the property, reviewing financial data, and studying the local market trends. A thorough analysis enables you to make educated judgments while avoiding costly blunders.

For example, if you see a home offered below market value, you may be tempted to make an offer right away. However, a comprehensive inspection and research of comparable sales in the neighborhood can identify potential red flags, like as needed repairs or zoning difficulties. Taking the time to consider these things will help you avoid unexpected charges in the future.

Forming a Reliable Team

Scaling up your property buys also entails broadening your professional network. Building a dependable team of specialists, such as real estate agents, property managers, contractors, and financial consultants, is critical. These specialists may offer useful insights, assist with property management, and guide you through the complexities of real estate transactions.

For example, a professional real estate agent can assist you in identifying homes that meet your investment criteria and negotiating advantageous conditions.

Similarly, a qualified property manager can streamline processes, ensuring that your buildings are well-maintained and consistently profitable.

Looking into Creative Financing Options

As you pursue future purchases, consider inventive financing solutions to broaden your options. Traditional bank loans are not the only way to become a property owner. Consider alternatives include seller financing, partnerships, or using home equity lines of credit (HELOCs).

For example, if you have large equity in your existing properties, you can use it to fund additional acquisitions. This method can offer you with the necessary funds without requiring a large capital investment. Seller financing can also be a win-win situation because it allows you to negotiate better terms directly with the seller.

Developing a Growth Mindset

Finally, developing a growth mindset is critical as you increase your investments. Accept challenges and see setbacks as learning opportunities. The real estate market can be unpredictable, but keeping a good attitude and a willingness to adapt can help you stand out from less resilient investors.

For example, if a specific investment does not perform as planned, investigate the scenario to see what went wrong. Adjust your strategy based on your findings and continue to look for new prospects. Building money through real estate is a journey, and staying focused on your long-term objectives can yield enormous returns.

Scaling up by acquiring additional properties in real estate investing is an effective approach for accumulating wealth and reaching financial independence. Understanding the benefits of diversity, assessing your financial capacity, and completing rigorous due diligence can allow you to make informed selections that line with your objectives.

Long-Term Strategies for Financial Freedom

To achieve financial freedom through real estate investing, you must not only take a smart approach to property purchase, but also commit to long-term planning. By adopting deliberate tactics and focusing on long-term growth, investors can build a strong portfolio that delivers income for years to come. This chapter delves into important long-term measures that can help you achieve financial freedom.

Developing a Vision for Your Financial Future

Any great investing strategy is built around a clear vision. Understanding what financial independence means to you—whether it's retiring early, touring the world, or simply living comfortably—allows you to create clear, attainable goals. This vision acts as the cornerstone for your long-term plan, directing your actions and keeping you motivated.

Consider the case of Sarah, a mid-career professional who hoped to retire by 55. Sarah defined her vision and set specific targets, such as obtaining three rental homes within ten years. This clarity enabled her to concentrate on identifying properties that would create enough income flow and grow over time, eventually bringing her closer to her retirement goal.

Developing a Diversified Portfolio

Diversification is an important investment idea that reduces risk while increasing rewards. When extending your portfolio, consider adding a variety of properties, including residential, business, and even short-term rentals. This strategy not only diversifies your risk across markets, but it also taps into a variety of revenue streams.

For example, if you own single-family houses in suburban communities, investing in a commercial property in a rising location can help you balance your portfolio. While residential properties may undergo seasonal swings in occupancy, business leases typically offer longer terms and greater consistency. Similarly, short-term rentals might benefit from travel trends, providing larger returns during peak seasons.

Adopting a Buy-and-Hold Strategy

A buy-and-hold approach has been shown to be an

effective way to develop wealth in real estate. This strategy is purchasing properties with the purpose of keeping them for the long term, enabling appreciation and rental income to compound over time.

For example, John paid $250,000 for a duplex in a developing neighborhood. Instead of selling it after a few years, he kept it while the area expanded significantly. Over a decade, the property increased to $400,000, and John earned constant rental income during that time. This technique not only increased equity but also generated cash flow, which he could reinvest in more properties.

Leveraging Passive Income Streams

One of the most tempting parts of real estate investing is the opportunity for passive income. As you grow your portfolio, prioritize properties that offer steady rental income, allowing you to reinvest earnings in future purchases or retirement savings.

Consider buildings that appeal to long-term tenants, such as those near schools or significant companies. For example, an apartment complex near a university can generate consistent demand for rental units, ensuring that your cash flow stays solid even during economic downturns.

Furthermore, looking into alternate revenue streams, such as storage units or billboards on your land, might provide an extra layer of financial security. Diversifying your revenue streams provides a safety net that helps you achieve your long-term wealth-building goals.

Understanding Market Cycles

Real estate is naturally cyclical, and knowing market trends is critical for making sound investment decisions. You may position yourself to capitalize on good situations by constantly tuned in to economic indicators such as interest rates, job rates, and housing demand.

For example, in a buyer's market, when property prices are low, you can buy more houses at a bargain. In contrast, in a seller's market, keeping onto your properties allows you to benefit from greater demand and rising prices. Recognizing these cycles allows you to optimize your investment approach, ensuring that you take advantage of every opportunity.

Investing In Property Management

As your portfolio increases, competent property management becomes critical to ensuring profitability. Whether you manage your properties yourself or engage a professional management company, the goal is to keep your investments running smoothly and efficiently.

Consider the example of Maria, who initially managed her properties on her own. While she appreciated the hands-on approach, she quickly recognized that the duties of tenant management and maintenance were too much. By hiring a property management company,

Maria was able to devote more time to acquiring new properties and developing her investment plan. This investment in management boosted her income flow while also increasing tenant satisfaction, resulting in greater retention rates.

Continually Educate Yourself

The real estate market is always changing, and remaining current is critical for long-term success. Commit to ongoing knowledge by attending workshops, reading industry journals, and networking with other investors. This continuous learning process may uncover new investing methods, market trends, and fresh opportunities.

For example, joining a local real estate investment organization allows you to share your experiences and learn from the triumphs and problems of others. This collaborative setting not only boosts your education but also your professional network, which can lead to prospective partnerships or mentorship opportunities.

Creating a succession plan

As you accumulate money through real estate, it is critical to consider your legacy. Creating a succession plan guarantees that your investments and financial goals are passed down to subsequent generations. This plan should specify how your property will be managed and transmitted in the event of retirement, illness, or death.

Consulting with financial experts and estate planning professionals can assist you in developing a thorough strategy that protects your assets while also carrying out your wishes. Taking these steps not only secures your financial future, but also provides piece of mind for you and your loved ones.

Developing a Long-Term Mindset

Finally, having a long-term attitude is essential for managing the ups and downs of real estate investing. Accept setbacks as opportunities for growth, and be patient as your investments appreciate over time. Building wealth is a marathon, not a sprint, and being committed to your vision will eventually lead to financial freedom.

For example, instead of panicking during a market downturn, remember the historical resilience of real estate. By retaining your properties and continuing to invest strategically, you can emerge from difficult times with increased wealth and prospects.

Implementing long-term strategies for wealth creation and portfolio expansion is critical on the path to financial freedom. You may confidently handle the complexity of real estate by establishing a clear strategy, diversifying your investments, and committing to ongoing education. Adopting a long-term perspective prepares you for long-term success and financial independence.